The Exchange Manifesto

How organised markets sustain development throughout the world

Patrick L Young

Derivatives Vision Publishing

By the same author:

Books:

Capital Market Revolution
New Capital Market Revolution
The Promiscuous Investor
Single Stock Futures – A Traders Guide
An Intangible Commodity (Editor)

White papers (include):

Megatrends in Finance

This book is copyright©Patrick L Young 2007

No Reproduction Without Written Permission
of the Publishers

Published by Derivatives Vision

All rights reserved; no part of this publication may be reproduced, stored in a retrieval system, or transmitted in any form or by any means, electronic, mechanical, photocopying, recording, or otherwise without either the prior written permission of the Publisher or a license permitting restricted copying in the United Kingdom issued by the Copyright Licensing Agency Ltd, Saffron House, 6-10 Kirby Street, London EC1N 8TS. This book may not be lent, resold, hired out or otherwise disposed of by way of trade in any form of binding or cover other than that in which it is published without the prior consent of the Publisher.

First published 2007 as a limited edition (80 copies) to mark the AFM Tenth Anniversary in Buenos Aires, Argentina.

This is the First Public Edition, Published May 2007.

ISBN 978-99949-22-34-5

For all discussion as to rights please email:
Patrick@DerivativesVision.com

To Beata

Acknowledgements

The genesis of this tome has been somewhat frantic and all too brief. At the Istanbul (9th annual) AFM conference in May 2006, AFM General Secretary Krisztina Kasza floated the idea of a book. Within a week or so the germ of an idea occurred to me concerning a manifesto for markets to discuss in practical terms key issues relating to exchanges and indeed why they existed and why they need to exist.

The search for sponsors began soon after and we are delighted that various AFM members and supporters have banded together to fund the publication of this tome. To all the sponsors, we offer our thanks for being so generous, helpful and supportive of this project.

> Dubai Gold & Commodity Exchange
> EUREX
>
> Deutsche Borse Systems
> Euronext.LIFFE
> JSE SAFEX
> KELER
> MEXDER
> Multi Commodity Exchange
> NYBOT
> NYMEX
> OMX
> Options Industry Council
> RTS "Russian Trading System"
> SFOA

No Acknowledgement could begin without a sustained reference to Kriszti Kasza who is a pleasure to work with and maintains order amongst the disparate members of the AFM with charm and courtesy. Rod Gravelet-Blondin has been a constant source of encouragement to the whole enterprise.

Ultimately, having written this book in what amounts to a remarkably condensed period of time, my thanks go to Sigurd Hogsbro for always good naturedly ensuring my IT works wherever I seem to be. Mark Blundell, Mike Charlton, "Kip" Cheseldine and Steve

Heuser, remain constant sources of amusement and inspiration. Colin Howard was especially helpful in providing various pieces of documentation which served me well with templates for the technology section in particular. Sabine Ferber and Peter Velati remain a great help, thank you all.

Naturally, there is, as ever, a special mention to my Mum. Meanwhile my team of leading supporters namely Beata Traczykowska, Laura Romanska and Laura Shumiloff must be thanked profusely for their unstinting support. It is sad to note that my good friend Lutzifer Lor Matisse Shumilov died as this book was preparing for publication. As ever the staff of CapoCaccia/CapoSushi (Clara, Barbara, Loris, Carmelo and "Chef" Kazuo) have taken great interest in the gestation of this project...

Finally a word of thanks to Lynne Spaight who stepped in at the last minute to save the day with my typesetting when my initial typesetter was taken ill and unable to complete this project.

It only remains to note that all errors, omissions and faux pas are mine (both having written the book and overseen its publication).

Feedback relating to the book will be welcome and can be sent to ply@erivatives.com

Contents

Foreword	1
Preface	4
Introduction	10
The Benefits of Exchange Markets	26
A Brief History of Exchange Markets	36
Core Product Concepts A Simple Primer	48
Infrastructure/Requirements & Technology to Create a Market	62
Clearing & Confidence The Great Imperative	74
Education & Market Regulation Achieving an Equilibrium	86
Competition/Prospects & Development	94
Conclusion	100

Foreward

Celebrating the 10th Anniversary of the the Association of Futures Markets

Dear Reader,

It seems remarkable that we are celebrating the 10th anniversary of the Association of Futures Markets by returning to our birthplace, Buenos Aires.

The AFM has proven a dynamic group dedicated to the process of creating a greater exchange presence world wide with particular emphasis on the benefits of exchanges, and especially derivatives exchanges, in the emerging markets of the world.

The exchange business has changed remarkably during the past decade and at the AFM we have now benefited from many new members who were not in existence at the time of our foundation.

We look forward to the next ten years of growth with excitement and anticipation. The prospect of consolidating the benefits provided by electronic trading are matched by the prospect of better markets helping more farmers, financiers and traders to benefit from a growing range of products.

We hope you will enjoy this book, which we see as a form of manifesto about the exchange itself. It has been written by Patrick L Young and we thank him for the time he has devoted to this interesting project which we hope will further encourage discussion and debate about the future of the marketplace. Finally, we thank our General Secretary Krisztina Kasza for her sterling work in maintaining the organisation of the Association and in helping to produce this book.

With best wishes,

Jose Klein,
Retired Chairman, Mercado a Termino de Buenos Aires

Szergej Keresztesi,
Chairman, Budapest Commodity Exchange

Mircea Filipoiu, CEO & President, Romanian Commodities Exchange

Gergely Horvath,
CEO & President, Central Clearing House and Depository Ltd (Budapest)

Vladislav Streltsov,
President, RTS Stock Exchange, Russia

Gyorgy Dudas, CEO & President, Central Clearing House and Depository Ltd (Budapest)

Hamdi Bagci,
CEO, Turkish Derivatives Exchange

Ricardo Marra,
Chairman, Mercado a Termino de Buenos Aires

Preface

Any market, whether new or established, needs to have a regular dialogue with not merely its users but also all those who may be affected by its activities. To this end, government, the media and indeed regulators are a vital first step.

The Exchange Manifesto

Preface

"Free Trade is God's Diplomacy. There is no other certain way of uniting people in the bonds of peace."

Richard Cobden

There are those who will argue that there is nothing new under the sun. To some extent they are right. In many respects the precepts and concepts by which so many items on Planet Earth have been created were discussed or at least hypothesised by thinkers decades or centuries ago. The writings of Jules Verne or before him, Leonardo Da Vinci give two significant attestations to the creativity of the human mind and its innate ability to create remarkable inventions.

Nevertheless, during the last century the world has witnessed a pace of development in technology which is simply breathtaking. There are those who may be detractors of cars or air travel or computers or the technology that is nowadays commonplace in food preparation and storage but that is surely to miss the core point. The convenience and enhancement of living standards has been available to vast numbers of the world's population and even those who are unable to partake of all the luxuries to be found in the most developed nations are nonetheless privy to the opportunity of working in industries that give them a sound living standard thanks to the world's technological development.

Yes, there may be a long way to go but gradually the world of technology extends throughout the globe and in fact the ability to leapfrog certain technologies (for instance through adapting mobile telephone networks as opposed to fixed line connectivity) is enabling many people the world over to actually trade in markets from their mobile phones in a way which was unthinkable

The Exchange Manifesto

even for the Rockefellers a century ago.

Ah yes, exchange markets.

I have always been fascinated by the world of exchange markets and so this is for me not just a manifesto for an intriguing industry that can enrich and enhance the lives of many, but also a personal manifesto to discuss the changes that have been brought upon this industry in recent years and how that has led to remarkable progress and a wonderful new world of markets. There are those who believe that markets are the preserve of the limousine-driving, private jet-using classes. I sincerely hope this book will prove quite the contrary. In fact the old fashioned club apartheid of many markets has been swept away in a fashion embracing not merely meritocracy but a remarkably level playing field enabling access for just about anybody anywhere in the world.

That is not to say that markets are an unregulated free-for-all – quite the contrary. Rather this is a book abut how that core unit of commerce, the exchange, is making a stunning comeback from a fusty industry where few entrepreneurs really wanted to get involved, into a dynamic industry which itself is both a pivotal player in and also a key enhancer of, the least frictional methods of creating transactions.

In many respects the world of the exchange, as we will see, changed little for centuries. Suddenly during the past decade various issues came together to create an explosion. This process I christened the "Capital Market Revolution." The powers of globalisation and deregulation have had a guiding hand in this whole process but it is the vast, explosive growth in computing, network technology and indeed that most famous of networks - the internet - which has sped the exchanges from being a rather dull bunch of clubs into remarkable powerhouses of capitalism.

My own interest in exchanges has now included nearly 20 years working around them in some way or another, as a broker, an analyst, a trader both on floors and via electronic screens, as well as an advisor to exchanges, governments, and a myriad of different bankers and intermediaries. It has been a fascinating time and this manifesto is an attempt to distil in a simple fashion the core precepts of just why exchanges are so significant at present and just how regions or nations can go about best implementing them as a tool for providing significant enhancements to the developments of markets.

This book has been commissioned as a result of my suggestion via the Association of Futures Markets, an organisation which in so many ways epitomises the core of the modern-day exchange. Each year a core group of about 100 people meet to discuss the issues surrounding the development of their markets, in all manner of commodities, interest rate and equity products, as well as many other exotic items in the derivatives firmament. Some members are parts of enormous cash and derivatives hybrid exchanges, others represent perhaps a handful of people. At its core, the Association of Futures Markets exists to promote the exchange business as a means for the enrichment of society, as a driver of growth and a means to encourage sustainable economic development. When their indefatigable General Secretary Krisztina Kasza suggested the concept of a book at their Istanbul conference, to mark their 10th anniversary event in March 2007, a period of thought led me to realise that what would be best was in fact a Manifesto for Exchanges. There is no single tome which neatly and readably discusses the nature of the who, what, where and perhaps most significantly why, of exchanges.

Therefore, this book was born. The project has been funded by a series of sponsors to whom we are very grateful and I have written the book for no upfront fee in an effort to ensure that it was produced. The core readership of this book is broad, so some experienced market practitioners may wish to skip some paragraphs. At the same time, in a multi-asset class world with new product exploding in just about every direction, the difficulty in such a tome is cramming in sufficient information to interest the practitioner while not intimidating the non-practitioner. A key marketplace for this book is amongst students of markets and in particular regulators, governments and so forth who want an easy-to-digest guide to the often bewildering financial marketplace.

Exchanges are at their core remarkably simple but with a dizzying scope of technological process, they can appear somewhat complex. The exchange industry itself has not been exactly helpful, often trying to make the industry look a great deal more complex than it truly is. The driving factor for this book is to provide a basis of understanding concerning the workings of exchanges and their advantages for all citizens of all nations whether at the richest end of the G7, or indeed the per capita poorest of emerging markets. This book is aimed at everybody with an interest in understanding the benefits of exchange markets including all those involved in the industry (or considering an exchange business): politicians, regulators, the media and students. I hope you will all find this a concise and useful guide to understanding the overwhelming benefits of exchanges in providing economic growth for all.

I have presumed some knowledge of financial market jargon as I doubt this will be the first financial publication readers will have picked up. Hopefully, concepts such as the bid/offer spread are familiar but if not, I would encourage you to "google" any of the multitude of glossaries available online which may help you to understand this tome.

It is vital to educate government, the media and regulators and keep them updated about our markets. Nobody has ever produced a genuine pocket-sized guide to just why our markets are vital in all economies. I believe that this slim volume will become a classic publication which will help promote AFM and its marketplaces as well as providing a welcome tool to promote exchange market and derivatives literacy in the world.

Introduction

If your country has a record of restrictions on capitalism then don't be surprised when it's the keen students of deregulation that win the prizes. Similarly, close your markets in any way and your population will eventually find the lure of fighting it out with North Korea at the bottom of the global misery indices largely unappealing.

The Exchange Manifesto

Introduction

"Trade is the wealth of the world:
Trade makes the difference between one nation and another;
Trade nourishes Industry, Industry begets trade;
Trade dispenses the Natural Wealth, which Nature knew nothing of."

Daniel Defoe

The essence of markets like most essences of civilisation centres upon community. Hubs have evolved and disappeared throughout history. Trading centres have given way to the contemporary term "financial centre" but in fact there is little difference between their core facilities which have involved a clustering of brokers and traders allied with a physical location on a known trade route. Such "clusters" devoted to the trading or development of a particular product or group of products have risen and fallen and even disappeared. Few nowadays talk about the Silk Road city of Ctesiphon yet here a massive kernel of dealing took place in silks and other commodities. When the pattern of the Silk Road changed, the city itself ultimately disappeared.

Transport has of course played a huge role in the development of markets and it was the explosion in intercontinental shipping that led to the establishment of the first series of modern contemporary stock markets, many of which are still in existence.

From the 17th century, merchants clustered alongside entrepreneurs and speculators to alter their risk profiles in a fashion which helped with the exhilarating prospect of developing commerce between the existing nations and those of the new worlds of exciting foreign territories located at the fringes of Europe, throughout Asia, Africa and the Middle East and, of course, in the Americas.

Excess and Irrational Exuberance

Since the earliest days of markets, there have been booms and busts. The Tulipomania, South Sea and Mississippi bubbles affected markets in Holland, Britain and France several centuries ago while the twentieth century was marked by several crashes in major world markets including those on Wall Street in 1929 and much of the world in 1987.

Prices can overheat and markets, being driven by a dynamic related to human emotion, will have a tendency to over-react to events (both up and down!). In this respect, governments need to understand that there is only a limited amount they can do. Certainly bad government such as fuelling high inflation or issuing excessive levels of government debt, will encourage markets to punish you. For all the railings of politicians about illicit foreign speculators, there are no clear historical examples where markets have crashed because the government was in fact perfectly competent.

Markets are self-correcting mechanisms. True, markets have a tendency to excess on occasion but they also have a capacity for spotting value. Therefore, a huge run on a currency which is fundamentally unjustified will soon be ended with a rush of value seeking investors keen to buy below what they perceive as good value.

Therefore anti-crash risk management remains one more of precaution than direct action. Maintaining a reasonable equilibrium in the economy will help promote markets but on occasion when they do overheat, while government and central banks can make some effort to calm things down (e.g. through public statements and prudent direct action in accepted monetary policy instruments), ultimately there may be occasions where markets career somewhat out of control. At this stage, it may be worrying for government but unfortunately cycles will out and bursting bubbles without an explosion is a subject for several volumes in itself. A sound, transparent exchange-based mechanism at least ensures that credit ought to remain sounder than is the case where a traded product relies on a less opaque system, or has no central counterparty clearing mechanism to rely on.

The exchange industry itself has in fact remained largely unchanged throughout history – until recently. The activities in marketplaces of antiquity (whether in Greece, Rome, or Egypt to name but three examples) seem to have created a blueprint which remained largely true throughout the world and whose core principles were used for the establishment of what have become the greatest markets in modern times, in New York, Chicago and London amongst other cities.

Originally, small groups of interested parties clustered in markets to trade livestock and commodities. There is evidence that forward settlement was available hundreds and indeed thousands of years ago.

The current cornerstone markets of the world, such as the London Stock Exchange, were born from transactions driven in the coffee shops of London where in and around Throgmorton Street, there was daily trading. Regulars were able to reserve their seats in the most appropriate places in the bars and as they tasted the exciting new beverages created by continental coffee beans, ships and their cargoes were traded. From this business (which was also significantly large in Amsterdam), the coffee shops gradually gave way to more organised exchanges which were structured like clubs with criteria for the election of members. Soon, markets existed in most major European cities. Simultaneously, some people preferred to use alternative means to alleviate the risk on their shipping cargoes and this created the precepts of the modern insurance business.

Of course imperial politics were key and the most significant deals with the colonies in the Americas and India for instance were driven from London. In Amsterdam, transactions tended to favour nations such as Indonesia as well as many local commodity products from around the lowlands. Soon with a stock exchange in every city, merchants were able to enjoy a more stable potential outcome and the economy developed rapidly in many areas.

All development happens with some setbacks and stock markets were not immune to these (see sidebar: excess and irrational exuberance) but generally the presence of organised exchange markets has helped citizens by allocating scarce resources more efficiently and permitting business expansion by all citizens.

The Exchange Manifesto

Let us be clear however that this is not a polemic devoted to rampant capitalism. Certainly a great many aspects to how capitalism developed are not widely accepted today and a balance had to be sought to ensure that workers were not exploited in the process of making factory owners rich and so forth. The key point is that the stock market enabled great wealth to be created. Vast numbers of people found gainful employment thanks to the activity of exchanges in providing a marketplace where money could be sent to the projects which were deemed most of interest to the benefit of speculators. While the riches of the few are frequently of interest as tabloid media fodder, it cannot be disputed that open stock markets are a marvellous means of creating widespread employment and national wealth.

The only major change in stock exchange development before the modern age came during the 19th century. The invention of the telegraph suddenly meant that brokers, investors and traders could find out about price changes and market movements far beyond the reach of their city with immediacy. This completely changed the equation of exchanges and suddenly the implied internationalisation of markets became a genuinely global spectre of prices.

In the USA every city had created a stock exchange but with the advent of the telegraph very soon the major markets polarised. With the exception of Chicago which was a major hub for commodity trading (with a stock exchange too), most of the trading polarised on the coasts, in the west in San Francisco and in the east in Philadelphia and New York.

Similarly, in Europe many exchanges began to concentrate on one area. In the post World War Two era, exchanges in the UK were brought together under the London Stock Exchange banner as increasing telephone access allowed business to be pooled at one point of central liquidity in each country. This has tended to be the pattern across the world although some countries such as Germany retain various regional exchanges. Nevertheless, one national exchange tends to have the lion's share of the overall business (e.g. Frankfurt in Germany).

Therefore, the exchange business changed little for hundreds, if not thousands of years. Certainly, the organisation and governance structure along with the methods of dealing on most exchanges, would have been easily recognisable to a trader from centuries earlier (qv. Confusiones da Confusiones).

The late 20th century started to bring radical upheaval to the exchange business. A series of events continue to transform the business in ways that were simply not foreseen a decade or two previously.

It may seem remarkable to some but originally stock exchanges had an agreed fixed commission rate. So, while we are used to supermarkets or other businesses being able to compete on price as well as service and so on, with stockbroking, all charges were fixed. This may strike readers as being somewhat oxymoronic that the supposed cutting edge of capitalism was in fact ruled by a rather Stalinist concept of price flexibility. The Republican government under President Richard Nixon in the USA was the first major nation to grasp the mettle and in 1975 the New York Stock Exchange began the process of deregulation.

Deregulation has been increasingly common throughout major markets. Perhaps not surprisingly, the UK under the reforming zeal of Prime Minister Margaret Thatcher undertook a major reform of exchange practices and thus old fashioned monopolistic specialities in broking, market making and issuing were done away with and modern securities practice permitted the creation of large integrated firms dealing with all aspects of the stock market food chain.

In the midst of this process, another subtle sea change was taking place. The increasingly deregulated financial markets led to an explosion in the construction of new ways to manage risk. Thus the modern derivatives movement was born and with it the most exciting tools in financial history began revolutionising the world of finance.

Derivatives
The derivatives marketplace has in fact been around for thousands of years. The concept of taking delivery of a commodity at a future date for a price fixed now has long traditions in most commodity dealing nations. Modern derivatives markets started to spring up in the American Midwest in the 19th century and began revolutionising the prospects for producers who wished to hedge their commodity positions against their crops. Gradually

The Exchange Manifesto

the conventional cash and forward markets gave way to commoditised future and options markets where everybody could participate in the marketplace with equal access (see sidebar).

The initial phase of US market deregulation coincided with the death of the Bretton Woods system of currency relationship and the US dollar began freely floating against other currencies. Allied with other deregulatory measures this created the greatest sea change in financial markets with the growth and widespread adoption of the derivatives markets.

Initially there were futures and options on foreign exchange launched in the USA which then led to the growth of futures on Treasury Bonds and interest rates in the USA and subsequently the creation of stock index futures which tracked baskets of stock values.

This effectively created a third dimension in the marketplace (see box below).

Derivatives: friend or foe?

There have been many critics of the derivatives market since their expansion into financial products during the 1970s. Headlines often shriek about the perils of derivative instruments.

Yet, in reality, the off balance sheet market has made a significant change for the better in risk management. The world of derivatives has given way to a marketplace which is truly a derivatives world.

Yes, derivatives represent a more complex, intangible product with many potential payoffs. However, derivatives are already available at every level of society although many of those using derivatives may not even realise they hold such products. Good examples here are lenders (especially mortgagees) whose interest rates are fixed at low levels for fixed periods of time – this is usually achieved through swap and similar markets to keep the interest rate hedged. Derivatives have made the traditional staple floating interest rate mortgage (commonplace in multiple jurisdictions with the significant exception of the USA) a much less stressful exercise for many folk the world over.

> The irony is that derivatives are now being used by people throughout the world who probably think they are too dangerous to benefit from their power. As I write, more people hold mortgages which have had their interest rate fixed through derivatives product hedging than actually traded all derivatives markets in history until 1990.
>
> Nowadays derivatives are a key part of the financial firmament. As I often like to note, this is "a derivatives world." The derivatives markets add strength and depth to the underlying cash markets as well as providing an added dimension to the business of trading: the ability to hedge positions through a wide-ranging array of methods – which allows everybody from banks and large financial institutions through to essentially subsistence farmers in India to hedge the future price of produce and thus lock in a guaranteed return. Such guaranteed returns do not merely help ensure prosperity, they permit subsistence farmers to escape the poverty trap.
>
> Naturally, derivatives products require user education before they can be used. Then again farmers cannot expect to use sophisticated farm machinery without some element of training. The simple understanding of derivatives products can be grasped by all those who can manage other simple tenets of modern life such as democracy or income tax. While many products can be misused to cause problems, in the case of derivatives, the benefits by far outweigh the potential problems. Welcome to the derivatives world.

As we mentioned, the key issue with the exchange marketplace was the use of face-to-face or "open outcry" dealing methods. This involved numerous variations around a key theme of specific locations assigned to specific markets and brokers, traders and so forth all standing where they wanted to get the best opportunity to use that marketplace.

The open outcry marketplace was still being trumpeted as the best model by many people well into the 1990s despite the fact that the writing on the wall had arguably been evident for nearly as long as currencies had been free-floating. A plan for an electronic exchange was touted by the man regarded as the "father of financial futures" Dr Richard Sandor when he was still a Pro-

OTC versus exchange

The derivatives business has traditionally had two distinct types of product. Exchange products tend to be commoditised and accessible by anybody with the financial wherewithal who meets appropriate regulatory standards. Institutions seeking bespoke solutions have traditionally dominated in the OTC market.

A key distinction for these products in addition to their commoditisation versus bespoke nature is that OTC products tend to be traded bilaterally (relying on the credit standing of the counterparties) while exchanges involve the use of a clearing mechanism ("clearing house") which effectively alleviates the risk of trader A going bust and not delivering his cash or commodity to trader B before settlement. (i.e. the clearing house is the counterparty to every buyer and seller from a risk management perspective). Thus an exchange market with a sound clearing system benefits from many financial safeguards as well as being accessible to even the smallest trader. OTC markets, on the other hand, tend to be the exclusive preserve of only the highest credit rated institutions.

OTC markets have made great innovations in trading. Exchange markets are widely acknowledged by practitioners, governments and regulators as being the safer option for markets – especially developing markets, thanks to their strong clearing infrastructure and democratic pricing (i.e. one price is essentially available to all exchange participants).

Nevertheless, it remains better to have both exchange and OTC markets. To have neither suggests a moribund totalitarian apology for an economy.

fessor on the West Coast of America. Various fledgling electronic exchanges including one in Bermuda (INTEX) stuttered and failed to gain traction. Nevertheless, it started to become evident to most onlookers that the future was electronic some years before the dawn of the 21st century. In this respect, the Australian Stock Exchange is notable for moving away from its floor to an electronic system in 1987 (ironically what turned out to be Black Monday, October 19th, 1987 had seemed an inconspicuous date to choose at routine planning meetings more than half a year earlier). Nevertheless, in the fast and furious world of trading, the concept of electronic dealing was seen as at best a way of extending opening hours by most leading exchanges. The German DTB (later to merge with SOFFEX of Switzerland and create EUREX) led the way in proving that in fact electronic trading methods were much more practicable and cost effective for all parties concerned.

Just as EUREX was steamrollering the open outcry opposition in Europe (the competition ultimately turned electronic and grew to flourish once again, incidentally), so too another intriguing development in the world of computing was gaining ground which would ultimately revolutionise the exchange business – and indeed its profound effects will continue to impact the industry for some years to come.

The power of an exchange lies in three key capabilities:

- Its processing (i.e. transactional ability)
- Its network for distribution of product
- Its ability to settle and clear (in fact if the exchange is not seen as having sufficient financial probity then only suckers will go there – a simple example is between choosing to stuff your bank notes under the bed of a stranger or in a reputable bank – most sane folk will choose the safer option of the bank.

The power of the electronic trading system provides an incredible speed in pure processing power (providing of course the orders can be broken down into sufficiently simple building blocks to make the order easily transmissible and executable).

Moreover, an electronic exchange can attain great power through its network. This is not just the names of the people who are likely to deal (holding accounts as required at the exchange and so on) but also being able to access them easily.

With the birth of electronic networks, the ability to add somebody to the network meant they could then be a trader on that exchange (ceteris paribus – especially on the regulatory front) from anywhere in the world.

Of course for major exchanges, usage of a dedicated network is

The Exchange Manifesto

paramount for the world's largest investors and traders but then again thanks to that invention by Tim Berners-Lee at CERN, the World Wide Web has in fact propelled the concept of exchange provision to a point where a truly world class marketplace can be created in a box. The power of the network has come to any marketplace in the world, thus making the exchange an exquisite centre of the world of commerce in a way that means the local can be both the national and the international, truly global in scope, even within a very narrow niche...

Thus two major impacts upon the exchange business occurred during the latter years of the 20th century and the dawn of the second millennium.

Organised capital has been seen in some political circles as the enemy of the people yet one can argue that particularly in the current marketplace, the exchange concept has rarely been a greater friend of sensible development and the provision of stability for smaller players throughout world markets.

For many, the exchange in practice is what they see on financial television: the massive halls of the floor of the mercantile exchanges in Chicago or New York for instance. While a great concept until a decade or so ago, floor based markets have now been largely rationalised. While floors provide a fascinating show, their role in contemporary markets is diminishing rapidly. Emerging markets are generally finding they can export their skills base through cheaper manufacture of product or the provision of outsourcing services. It is not the sheer human capital which is the prerequisite for an exchange, rather it is modern technology which drives the contemporary exchange marketplace. It is now possible to establish a market to trade for a fraction of the cost required in previous generations. Moreover, that market can much more easily connect to a core trading hub in the world.

Therefore, one effect of IT has been both to shrink the world in its financial geography but also to expand the global opportunity when it comes to the ability of farmers or producers in one nation to trade with those on the other side of the world.

IT has created a flexibility in markets that has been a challenge to established regulatory structures. This has simultaneously ensured that no government can overstep the mark in terms of punitive regulations. Recently even the global superpower, the USA, has suffered financially as the Sarbanes Oxley Act, written in haste and driven by a revulsion at the crimes of Enron, has resulted in businesses suffering high costs of compliance. Many companies have simply moved their stock listings, or refused to list their stock in the US markets. Instead they have chosen other, more lightly regulated markets.

The world of exchanges was centred for centuries around not-for-profit clubs. In recent years, there has been a revolution in ownership structures. The Australian Stock Exchange was the first to make the move from mutuality to listing on its own stock exchange although it was the Swedish OM Group which first created a for-profit exchange during the 1980s.

In this book we will briefly review the history of exchanges and also peruse the concepts and precepts behind creating, running and regulating contemporary exchange markets. While written with an eye on the emerging markets of the world, nevertheless "The Exchange Manifesto" has been conceived as a tome which discusses the entire concept of exchange trading and to bring to as wide an audience as possible a general understanding of the benefits of exchange markets and how they are helping make commerce easier and thus raise living standards throughout the world.

The Exchange Manifesto title struck me when I considered the membership of the AFM itself. The strength of the Association nowadays lies in the many members it can count from amongst the former Warsaw Pact and other non-aligned communist countries. Their history in the 20th century was effectively dominated as a result of another (much more famous and it might be added better-written) tome, "The Communist Manifesto," constructed by the rather utopian bourgeois duo of Marx and Engels. It is richly ironic – and deeply painful – to note that as a result of the rather eloquent writings of Marx and Engels, more people have ultimately been killed than witnessed a considerable rise in their income. Ironically, even communism could not support itself without an urge to trade. The Soviet government operated a network of state banks in overseas territories in an effort to permit resource transfer. As a "doctrine of the emancipation of the proletariat", state-controlled communism has been an utter disaster. Without the benefit of market pricing, there remains little incentive to do anything amongst most social groups.

Therefore, given the global defeat of Communism (as measured by the collapse of the Berlin Wall and the birth of capitalist states throughout the former Soviet bloc), it seemed only appropriate to present this book as a manifesto of the Exchange itself – a core building block of capitalism at the epicentre of trade. The internet and IT has helped propel the exchange more than ever before to the epicentre of global trade and created a digital democracy of capital. Anybody anywhere in the world can increasingly access prices that were until recently only tradable amongst a select band of multinational institutions. The opportunity for even subsistence farmers to hedge their flowers, fruit and vegetables at the time of planting (and thus guarantee the return on their produce) has the potential to lift more farmers out of poverty in a single generation than have been aided by vast expenditure of cash and resources by multinational agencies during the 20th century.

Driving the ongoing process of deregulation, disintermediation and technology that I termed the Capital Market Revolution is the fact that we can now in this digital age recognise that the DNA of markets – the essential building block of all global commerce is what I term the "microtrade" – in other words a tiny transaction can now be made cost effectively in the global electronic marketplace.

In the year when Grameen Bank founder Muhammad Yunus became the first active financier to win the Nobel Peace Prize (2006), I began to write this tome. Grameen was a pioneering institution in the microloan business. Now we have reached the age of the profitable microtrade. That is a highly exciting prospect for everybody who is seeking to alleviate poverty and increase living standards throughout the world.

The business of the exchange may not appear at first sight to be a revolutionary activity but a key reason for this manifesto is indeed because I firmly believe that deployed sensibly, exchange markets can have a revolutionary effect on the lives of millions of ordinary people throughout the world. They may be homeowners whose mortgages have been hedged through derivatives markets or the subsistence farmers mentioned above. In every area of commerce, the removal of risks – whether price, commodity, credit, weather or any one of a multitude of other risks can produce incredible results in helping move an economy forward – and enrich the participants within that economy. This is a Manifesto for change promoting the modern incarnation of one of the oldest building blocks of trade throughout the world: the exchange.

In his compelling autobiography, Banker to the Poor, Muhammad Yunus concluded his preface in a fashion which neatly encapsulates my own feelings about the opportunities provided by exchanges in emerging markets:

"I want to tell this story because I want you to figure out what it means to you…I would like to invite you to join those of us who believe in the possibility of creating a poverty-free world and have decided to work for it. You may be a revolutionary, a liberal or a conservative, you may be young, or you may be old, but we can all work together on this one issue.

Think about it."

I did, I do and as a revolutionary in a suit, I am delighted to be the author of this, "The Exchange Manifesto" whose rallying call repeats the mantra of my earlier "Capital Market Revolution!"

"Liquidity! Accessibility! Transparency!"

Patrick L Young
Patrick@DerivativesVision.com

The Exchange Manifesto

Chapter one

The Benefits of Exchange Markets

A neat solution: exchanges help farmers choose the crops most in demand, raising supply and reducing the need for inefficient subsidies. Governments save, consumers save, farmers gain. No other mechanism manages to achieve such a tripartite success with so little friction.

The Exchange Manifesto

"Markets have broken free of states, and, of politics, and now girdle the globe…A prime cause of this shift is technological change, which has been accelerating at an ever more rapid pace."
Professor Jonathan Story

"The world is not the way they tell you it is."
Adam Smith

The history of all societies until now has been the history of trade. Class struggle may have appealed to a romantic few but in fact it has been the struggle to ensure a sufficient standard of living that unites everybody from a car dealer in modern day Belgrade to a primitive hunter gatherer in Bronze Age Britain. When mankind discovered a means to trade it opened the world to a richness of possibility, an opportunity for those with particular skills to specialise. By engaging in trade, they had the opportunity to sustain their own lifestyle and also collectively enrich society. There was no class struggle involved in major technological developments such as the wheel. Likewise, it was an expansionary desire for trade and colonisation that drove the origins of the stock markets which themselves had been built on the ancient practices of bringing excess produce to market where it could be traded for other services or in exchange for currency.

The common misconception in many circles remains that exchanges are clubs for rich men to transact business and profiteer with a blithe disregard for the benefit of humanity as a whole. The truth is that while self-interest naturally remains an ingredient in the mix, that self-interest is frequently closely allied to the need to achieve sustainable development. After all, markets thrive on more and richer participants. Market participants in a competitive international economy need to compete for scarce consumers and to that end find a means to make the exchange most beneficial for them.

Similarly, it is a common argument that derivatives products are somehow the devil's tools, highly sophisticated products that simply cannot be understood by normal humans (as opposed to the "rocket scientists" who create them) and are all aimed at adding risk to the portfolio of whoever ends up owning one.

Of course, there is always an element of truth in such accusations. At their most sophisticated, derivatives are indeed somewhat complex and certainly when they have been bought by less skilled investors (to whom they ought not to have been sold in the first place), some chaos can ensue.

Derivatives are rather like loaded weapons. If we allow a reckless adolescent access to one then it is likely that chaos will ensue. The scale of the damage will be different depending on whether that loaded weapon is a single shot air rifle, a revolver or a rocket propelled grenade.

There is scant evidence that derivatives actually cause any market malfunctions – rather they often tend to act as a counterbalance. In other words, many countries hold vast arsenals of weapons while remaining peaceful neighbours. It takes an outside factor such as an act of aggression, to provoke combat.

The most highly publicised trading problems encountered following derivatives usage have not been as a result of the derivatives themselves but rather due to poor management. Losses by rogue traders such as Nick Leeson at Barings and Yasuo Hamanaka at Sumitomo were not caused by their trading derivatives per se but rather because somehow or other the management apparatus failed in the provision of adequate risk controls.

The list of those who can benefit from exchanges is vast. For the sake of brevity I will provide two examples of professional groups which I imagine all readers are already somewhat familiar with: companies and governments.

Companies
Modern stock markets grew out of facilitating a market in the shares of joint stock companies, as a means of pooling risk amongst those companies dealing with new (to Europe anyway!)

territories. As exploration and the movement of commodities expanded in the 17th and 18th centuries, the original financing of such transit using patronage from ruling royal families began to be insufficient to finance new expeditions. The increasing demand for merchantable goods led to the foundations of the largest merchant classes in history.

Nowadays, stock markets help companies in several ways:

- permitting the listing of large existing companies on the stock market so facilitating dealing in their shares and also:
- permitting listed companies to list more shares (e.g. to allow them to redeem debt or to make acquisitions or fund other expansionary projects at a low cost.
- permitting companies to borrow money using bonds, convertible issues and so forth.

Governments are also permitted to borrow money through exchange markets. Derivatives in bond and bill contracts have helped make government refinancing significantly more efficient. This new efficiency (in just about everything from the overall interest rate of the bonds through to reductions in frictional dealing expenses) ultimately benefits citizens as any reduction in borrowing costs for government helps keep tax rates under control.

Particularly in recent times, markets for smaller companies than are typically seen on main stock exchange boards have been permitted on a series of "growth" markets such as London's AIM (Alternative Investment Market) and Plus Markets Group. Similar exchanges exist throughout the world and frequently they operate with a lower regulatory burden. This of course means the market may be slightly more risky for the average investor but by permitting companies to come to market sooner, it can significantly help increase growth in these companies, thus providing more jobs and profits.

Interestingly, such smaller capitalisation ("small cap") markets can often attract overseas companies – AIM in the UK has been particularly successful in listing overseas companies, especially from Russia for instance. Frequently such concerns grow up and blossom into businesses listed on the main board of a stock exchange.

The Exchange Manifesto

Smaller capitalisation stock markets provide an alternative to private equity. Developing company investors can use them to encourage corporate development while providing a value for that company relatively easily, thus enhancing transparency. This facilitates investment vehicles which have restrictions on holding non-quoted equity.

For the retail investor in particular, perhaps one of the greatest innovations in recent years has been organised funds listed on exchanges which track particular benchmarks or indices. The original term "index trackers" soon gave way to the slicker moniker "Exchange Traded Funds" or just "ETFs". Such funds have significantly reduced the costs of dealing for all investors, particularly retail ones. Old fashioned labour intensive mutual funds charged up to 5% (500 basis points) for selling out of a fund plus colossal management fees; ETFs rely on microtrade sized payment flows to mimic a benchmark with a bid/offer spread to enter and exit the fund which is minuscule by comparison with the old mutual funds. Moreover, ETFs permit constant dealing throughout the exchange's opening hours while mutual funds were traditionally redeemable only once per day (and then in a pricing formula which some investors felt favoured the fund at the expense of the investor).

Particularly spurred on by the booming commodity markets during this first decade of the 21st century, ETFs have also recently been listed on underlying commodities, enabling investors to trade or invest easily in gold or oil which can provide a sensible balance to portfolios which are otherwise holding considerable quantities of stock and require an inflation hedge.

The Exchange Traded Fund is truly the people's derivative. Traditional fund managers have charged fees on mutual funds where 500 basis points (5%!) was a typical bid/offer spread for the investor exiting a position. This was a huge cost and one which bore onerously on the private investors who could ill afford such substantial costs. With the advent of ETFs, investors are now able to gain access to a myriad of exposures in equity and commodity products world-wide for a modest brokerage cost and a tiny bid/offer spread often as low as a single penny. ETFs are born of a complex series of electronic microtrades with product packagers creating the ETF units using a minuscule commoditised payment structure. Thanks to being listed on exchanges, investors can check the value of their investment in real-time throughout the trading day if they so wish. Thus the old suspicions that the prices given by mutual fund operators at the end of the trading day may have favoured the institution at the expense of the individual have evaporated.

In the beginnings of commodity trading, the concept was to have a means to hedge crops and livestock when they were first planted or during what could often be a volatile gestation period as the vagaries of the weather (and the relative prices of other related commodities) impacted upon the price of any market. In those days hedging was complicated for those rural farmers some distance removed from the early telegraph stations.

True, even in modern times, there are agricultural co-operatives in remote parts of Eastern Europe where telephone lines and fax machines are still a rarity, requiring a secretary to transport orders by bus into the nearest village post office for a fax to be sent. However, with the growth of mobile communications and the ability of modern telephone systems to permit the transmission of data and voice together, commodities markets are coming alive in many parts of the world. In India, the pioneering work of exchanges such as the Multi Commodity Exchange (MCX) is already changing the work patterns of small farmers. The result is greater income and a concomitant reduction in the pressure of having to provide for their families in circumstances where only minor set-backs can turn into a subsistence problem.

MCX works hard to disseminate its prices through every possible means. Sophisticated electronic networks such as Reuters enable live, real-time prices to be sent to dealers all around the world, as well as being distributed for publication in newspapers and journals. At a simpler but nonetheless vital level, the MCX has a deal with the Indian Post Office so that MCX commodity prices are placed on notice boards displayed prominently in all major Indian towns. At only a modest cost, utilising the internet or mobile phones, farmers can transmit orders to the central MCX processors and thus hedge their crops. (On a systems note, MCX uses simple ubiquitous PC operating systems such as Windows (i.e not server architecture) to create their very reliable and scalable dealing technology.

There is already clear evidence of farmers checking MCX prices and then both hedging the highest priced markets and choosing to cultivate that particular crop. Thus high prices denote rising demand which the farmers endeavour to satisfy by growing that crop while at the same time the farmers know what their guaranteed income will be. This greatly assists with financial planning and reducing the stress levels of subsistence farmers accordingly. A neat solution: exchanges help farmers choose the crops most in demand, raising supply and reducing the need for inefficient subsidies. Governments save, consumers save, farmers gain. No other mechanism manages to achieve such a tripartite success with so little friction.

Admittedly, attempts to reproduce such hedging activities in the larger economies of the world have often been fraught. Anti-money laundering laws in the Western world require exchange users to provide corroboration of their very existence and their domicile such as copies of utility bills and photographic documents (passports/ID cards and so on) before they can access an exchange. Alas, in the outer zones of the Hindu cush and even many of the more fertile farming zones of Africa, there are entire farming co-operatives where nobody has ever received any such piece of identifying documentation.

Benefits to government
I have used this example before in several speeches and publications but it is such a perfect example I have no qualms about repeating it in this book for which it is ideally intended.

There are many nations which have organised central governmental boards to buy and supply a core commodity. The South African Maize Board undertook just such a process and each transaction cost the equivalent of 150 Rand per tonne of maize handled. Enter stage left the South African Futures Exchange which took up the reins of providing a direct hedging service to farmers when the Maize Board was finally condemned to closure. The frictional cost of a tonne of maize transacted on SAFEX Commodities as opposed to through the bureaucracy of the Maize Board has very tangible benefits to government, farmers, producers and consumers alike.

Electronic exchange markets are simply the cheapest means of facilitating commerce anywhere in the world. Equally they can provide a range of benefits to a greater diaspora of citizens and corporations than any other transactional method.

The world of electronic commerce has revolutionised the way many people buy goods the world over. In the consumer domain, eBay has become the 500 lb gorilla across the world (although there are strong competitors in some markets: QXL for instance is market leader in Poland). eBay may not have the same regulation as a financial market but it performs very similar functions – and as a means of reducing friction in commerce it has provided a remarkable revolution in both the new and second hand retail process.

Meanwhile the Alibaba website pioneered in Hangzhou China by Jack Ma has provided an exchange style platform which provides remarkably simple opportunities for commerce between suppliers in China (and elsewhere) with the rest of the world.

Whatever the platform, whatever way you look at it, the electronic platform has revolutionised online trading in all shapes and forms. Indeed, the impact of that revolution has barely begun to be felt. There are tangible benefits for everybody from companies of all sizes to individual investors. For governments, the benefits may not just be measured in the postive knock on effects on the first two groups but also in terms of a method of reducing government's own funding costs, eliminating transnational friction and promoting efficiency.

The Exchange Manifesto

www.ftindia.com

Pioneering Solutions, Empowering Exchanges.

Financial Technologies Group provides technological infrastructure and vertical market domain expertise to set up financial exchanges across equities and cash commodities, currency, debt and bond along with other specialized markets for precious metals, energy, carbon credits, real estate and online virtual world. Financial Technologies has complex project implementation capability which has been effectively used to set up exchanges successfully in a record time frame that have been profitable from the first day of operations.

Multi Commodity Exchange of India Ltd

Trade with Trust
India's No.1 Commodity Exchange

- India's largest commodity exchange is also globally the No.2 exchange in silver, No.3 exchange in gold and No.4 exchange in energy volumes.

Dubai Gold & Commodities Exchange

Dubai Gold & Commodities Exchange

- A 50:50 JV of Financial Technologies and MCX with Dubai Multi Commodities Center, DGCX was set up in a record 9 months.

IBS Forex

IBSFOREX

- Subscribed by over 25 banks, IBS Forex has achieved a cumulative turnover of about USD 40 billion till July 2006.

National Spot Exchange Ltd.

National Spot Exchange

- National Spot Exchange is a pan India electronic spot market for commodities, creating a bridge between physical market traders and derivatives markets.

Global Board of Trade

GBOT

- Financial Technologies has received an approval from the Financial Services Commission of Mauritius to set up a world class international multi commodity exchange.

Safal National Exchange of India Ltd.

SNX
SAFAL NATIONAL EXCHANGE

- Financial Technologies and MCX with Mother Dairy Foods have set up SNX to provide a nation-wide platform for trading in horticulture, floriculture, dairy and allied products.

FinancialTechnologiesExchangeSolutions
- CentralMatchingEngine
- CentralRiskManagementSystem
- OrderManagementSystem
- MarketInformationSystem
- BroadcastEngine, Clearing & SettlementSystem

Financial Technologies
Powering e-Xchange Markets

For more information, case studies and presentations write to us at marcom@ftindia.com

Chapter two

A Brief History of Exchange Markets

As the opportunities for trade grew with the colonies, so too the markets became effectively somewhat deregulated from the reach of the monarchy and the nascent private sector got involved.

The Exchange Manifesto

"Markets have existed as long as there has been a desire or need to exchange or trade commodities, irrespective of whether the population concerned was contained within a particular community, region, or dispersed internationally…"

David Courtney

The most powerful force in human history has been competition. No sport would survive without it and even in cerebral pursuits, where competition has been engendered it has brought great results for mankind. Jean-Dominique Cassini (born Giandomenico Cassini in Perinaldo, Italy) was funded by the court of the French King Louis XIV to discover new planets faster than the rival English court where Edmund Halley was Astronomer General at Greenwich. Similarly in markets, it has been the unleashing of competition which has been the biggest driving factor in the creation of wealth – widespread wealth at that, thanks to open markets. We will return to this issue of competition at a later juncture but first a brief discussion of the history of markets from the exchange perspective.

The original markets existed in commodities and there is evidence that in the bazaars of the silk road and in the agricultural and livestock markets of ancient Egypt, Greece and Rome to name but three significant empires, there were opportunities for traders not merely to transact produce for cash and immediate delivery but also forward contracts which existed to create an opportunity to buy (or sell) for delivery at a future date.

Thus derivatives markets had a foundation and such markets in fact often developed in splendid isolation: medieval rice markets in Japan for instance also had various kinds of forward contracts.

When the boom in exploration got going, initially the competition was between what were effectively national champions (sometimes foreign born such as Christopher Columbus), backed by the

The Exchange Manifesto

monarch. However, as the opportunities for trade grew with the colonies, so too the markets became effectively somewhat deregulated from the reach of the monarchy and the nascent private sector got involved.

Thus markets began to spring up in city centres, initially based in the new, fashionable coffee shops. Here traders in the likes of Paris, Amsterdam and London came together to hear the plans of entrepreneurs to import new products or to inhabit wondrous new territories for which they had secured the appropriate concession.

Soon coffee shops such as Jonathan's in London became the basis for a market in shares in the joint stock companies. By finding capital in this way, entrepreneurs were able to leverage and/or dissipate their risk in these projects. On a similar basis, those of a risk-oriented inclination could pop out of Jonathan's to the nearby Lloyd's coffee house where syndicates of individuals joined together to underwrite the risk of loss or damage (due to weather, piracy and other risks) to a cargo. Entrepreneurs could pay a premium and receive a policy to insure their goods. In this way the London Stock Exchange and the world's most famous insurance market were born within a few blocks of each other in the City of London.

The birth of speculation
Soon of course it became popular to speculate in the market in stocks and shares. An organised exchange was established in the Royal Exchange building (a marketplace spanning many centuries) while commodity trading operated from many places including Smithfield market where commodities included everything from horses to slaves in what was to put it mildly an often seedy place.

Nevertheless, markets provided capital to business and indeed then enjoyed some of the early speculative bubbles. An early example was the "Tulipomania" where the Dutch became fiscally obsessed with the arrival of tulip bulbs which became a "must have" fashion item of extraordinary degree (estates were sold against a particularly rare bulb). The French Mississippi and the UK South Sea Bubble each rocked the respective stock markets in the early 18th century when schemes to populate new regions and indeed pay off the national debt turned into crazed manias with many investors making vast profits while a huge number caught long at the top of the market ultimately lost a collective (and frequently individual) fortune.

The stock market itself survived and it has been plain to behavioural analysts of markets ever since that all markets go through cycles. While they need to have a deft touch, a key role of central bankers and governments is to endeavour to neatly prick speculative bubbles. That said, arranging a sensible deflation of bubbles is something which is invariably very difficult to achieve! On the other hand, market collapses are much simpler to provoke. Governments need only be seen to conspicuously remove confidence from the economy and free market (suddenly fixing floating currencies, imposing restrictions on forex transactions or loudly denouncing capitalist "conspiracies" and threatening foreign investors will usually successfully damage any economy).

Markets continued to develop their economies and in the early stages of the colonisation of the USA, exchanges began to crop up first in Philadelphia and New York (famously meeting under the Buttonwood tree in parkland near Wall Street) as well as throughout the country wherever a centre of commerce cropped up. In the middle of the nineteenth century as Europe was gripped by one of its periodic revolutionary years, 1848, the Chicago Board of Trade was founded to help farmers trade their produce. Coincidentally, 1848 was the last year that Europe suffered a widespread trans-continental crop failure with its concomitant food shortages and starvation.

With the birth of the telegraph, dealing in stocks, shares and commodities was somewhat revolutionised. For the first time it was no longer vital to be within the local town. Rather, stock trading began polarising, usually in the major commercial city. In larger nations such as the USA, they polarised on the coasts. The major US exchanges for instance became concentrated in San Francisco on the west coast and Philadelphia and New York on the eastern seaboard. For the first time, the telegraph meant that prices began to move across borders and even traverse continents. For instance, the prices of Liverpool cotton and all manner of stocks and commodities in London and elsewhere were used by the major US traders to frame their view on activities that day in the US markets. Likewise, it became possible for the elite to transact business across borders in a much more mellifluous fashion – although cross border equity transactions had been pioneered by the likes of the Rothschild family a century or more earlier. With the birth of the world wide web in the 1990s, the possibility for every global citizen to likewise enjoy "borderless" free trade was created.

The other significant development of the late 19th century was the birth of modern formalised derivatives markets with various exchanges such as the Chicago markets creating forward markets in a wide variety of commodities. This led logically to futures and options markets which have become so useful to all manner of interested parties today.

Overall, after the birth of the telegraph, while commodity derivatives gradually gained a foothold, the development of markets was relatively restricted. The stock market boomed in the 1920s on Wall Street and the subsequent crash was a massive event with share prices taking decades to recover. Nevertheless, it was not until the closing decades of the 20th century that the most significant developments began to take place in markets.

First came the deregulation wave. Historically bankers have tended to be notoriously poor as a collective group in discerning the best structure for market development. Indeed they tend to fight 'tooth and nail' the process of market change. This was certainly the case with the process of deregulation. It seems a complete absurdity to suggest that stockbrokers could not compete on price but in fact this was forbidden until the mid-1970's in the USA and some countries are still grappling with the implementation of this simple capitalist building block!

Yet the evidence is that where countries have got to grips with deregulation it has significantly enhanced their financial market structures, creating jobs within their financial organisations and equally helping lower the cost of raising capital, trading and hedging for all market participants.

The UK was the second major nation to deregulate, albeit a decade after the USA, thanks to Margaret Thatcher prompting the "Big Bang" in the City of London.

That said, this process of deregulating commissions and so forth was only a component of the momentous repercussions from the earlier death of the outmoded Bretton Woods system of essentially fixed foreign exchange rates amongst major trading nations. When Bretton Woods collapsed and foreign exchange trading became an open market, it was a glorious gift to good economies and provided a rude awakening to those nations whose economic stewardship was below par.

However, the real legacy of the Bretton Woods breakdown was to provide an incentive for intelligent minds to seek out ways to hedge the now more pressing three dimensional risks of modern markets. To this end, futures and options contracts began to be traded on exchanges in the USA devoted to foreign exchange products as well as other intangibles such as short term interest rates and bond markets. Individual stock trading was soon enhanced with the launch of options markets while stock index options and then futures gained traction soon after.

The most profound effect of these market changes was to create a whole new realm of opportunities to hedge risks and enhance speculative opportunities. That said, the modern futures and options markets (which began to gain ground from the 1980s) found themselves increasingly attracted to joining forces with the established stock markets which were often located only a few city blocks away in the major financial centres. A wave of mergers took place from the early 1990s in Europe and Asia. Particularly with the benefit of hindsight, it is still not entirely clear what the benefits of this rationalisation were for the derivatives markets which now provide the core of the profits growth in the integrated exchanges. The notion I floated at the time that "marrying your cousins does not necessarily improve the quality of the gene pool" has indeed been proven true – at least for the derivatives markets.

Nevertheless, that gets slightly ahead of our current narrative. For the 1980s and 1990s witnessed a massive growth in the marketplace for derivatives both on exchanges and in the more flexible (less regulated) Over The Counter (OTC) market. Derivatives product growth experienced a sudden and massive growth and this led to a massive explosion in capital markets world wide. While detractors began to emerge claiming that markets were endangered by the growth in derivatives products, no evidence has ever emerged to suggest that derivatives products make markets more volatile. Rather empirical evidence appears to point in precisely the opposite direction, that derivatives products can

The Exchange Manifesto

make markets a great deal safer for users through their provision of hedging possibilities.

While derivatives products were gaining ground, it was to be a technological revolution which would next power what have proven the two most dynamic decades in capital market development – and at the time of writing the second of these decades still has several years to run!

The rapid growth in new technology has literally torn apart the established means of dealing in global markets. The classic mode of floor trading, often involving individuals wearing brightly coloured jackets hand signalling and shouting at each other with "pits" devoted to particular products was proving a bottleneck in market development. As Moore's Law gradually continued on its merry way (with computer processor power doubling every 12-18 months), it became increasingly obvious that not only were electronic markets capable of trading greater volumes more rapidly (and with fewer operational inefficiencies) but also any benefits to human intermediation were lost to the accountants who sought to restrict costs, particularly those involving the often heady expenses of leading floor traders.

The initial major battleground for electronic versus open outcry trading was ultimately emphatically won by the German DTB/EUREX market. The London LIFFE marketplace was almost bankrupted in the aftermath. Many exchange managements panicked. Ironically, the new golden age of exchanges was just around the corner.

In addition to the growth of electronic processing power, the power of electronic networks was exploding. The internet was the most notable in the public eye but all of them provided the same threat/opportunity to markets.

Thanks to the growth in electronic markets, now every local or national exchange had the potential to operate across borders and be a competitor against any other international marketplace.

This incredible process further drove the whole concept of how an exchange needed to be run and thus accelerated an already growing vogue in exchange markets, namely the drive to demutualise the old fashioned exchange clubs and create new "for-profit" markets which listed their own shares on (frequently their own) exchanges. The Australian Stock Exchange was in the vanguard of demutualisation in the late 1980s while the process was much less popular in the USA and Europe. Nevertheless, various models have been utilised and the OM Group stands out as essentially a for-profit provider of exchanges throughout its history, having largely grown out of a highly successful technology vendor which to this day creates the software for many exchanges world wide. The UK market saw a move towards for-profit exchanges spurred by the near decimation of the UK LIFFE (financial futures) exchange by a head-on attack from the electronic for-profit Deutsche Terminbörse (part of Deutsche Börse and subsequently to be renamed EUREX as part of a merger with the Swiss SOFFEX). In the "Battle of the Bund" for dominance of the German (and consequently Eurozone) government bond futures/options market, DTB simply demolished the outmoded floor based trading model, prompting a widespread panic amongst marketplace operators throughout the world.

At the time of writing, some 20 exchanges worldwide are listed, ranging from the very tiny – the London Plus markets group (a dealing platform for larger stocks with origins as a small cap market) and the Australian National Stock Exchange (a tiny quasi-competitor to the (also) listed Australian Stock Exchange). Exchanges in Hong Kong, Singapore, Johannesburg and throughout Europe and the USA are publicly listed companies. Many more major exchanges will list in the near future as exchanges increasingly operate more like companies and less like club utilities for a limited group of users. The ramifications of the demutualisation process will continue to exacerbate tensions with some users, previously used to exerting considerable influence on exchange policy.

The growth of exchanges was in essence created not merely by the direct process of deregulation but particularly by the growth of derivatives products mentioned above.

As the marketplace has developed, just about any possible underlying has found itself spawning a derivatives product. Stock indices were created in the US in the 1970s and led to all manner of new methods for trading and investing which have had radical ramifications on the entire equity and funds management industry – effects which are still only beginning to really be felt now.

The Exchange Manifesto

It was with the growth of network technology providing the advantage to electronic trading methods that the product development revolution really began to gain ground. Put simply, electronic markets permit an exchange to introduce contracts much faster than was possible in the old mutual floor-based markets where traders needed to be found to man a pit (which itself had to be physically constructed) and so forth. Also, the net resources required to create a new contract are much fewer. Moreover, with new products taking up relatively cheap intangible digital silicone space on computers as opposed to seriously expensive downtown real estate, the golden age of product development has begun. In this respect, products can be both in new areas such as emissions or weather trading, or simply extensions of age old products such as agricultural commodities – and often regional specialities or different grades of products (such as crude oil or natural gas).

Overall, the history of the exchange has been one where customer demand has been driven by products which have invariably been declaimed as something approaching instruments of the devil. Yet within generations their position has become vital to the mainstream of finance (even though often the public may be ignorant of just what role they play – rather in the way that few motorists comprehend the effect their carburettors/fuel injection have on their car's performance and fuel efficiency).

The most significant issue for global financial markets remains the fact that the finance industry can provide elegant solutions to many problems, thus enhancing the business of commerce, providing government co-operates with a suitably elegant regulatory structure. This is a win-win situation which no government can afford to ignore.

Interest Rate Portfolio
More Choice

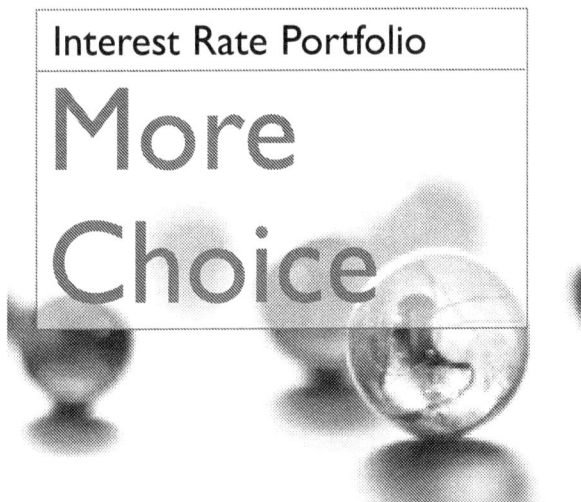

EURIBOR, Short Sterling, Euroswiss, Euroyen, Long Gilt, EuroMTS Bond Indices, Swapnote®

It's easier to trade interest rate futures and options contracts on Euronext.liffe.

We provide one trading platform, one set of rules, and access to one clearing house for the broadest portfolio of interest rate contracts of any derivatives exchange.

Trading interest rates on Euronext.liffe is simple, efficient and cost-effective.

To find out more visit www.euronext.com/derivatives, email stirs@liffe.com or call +44 (0)20 7379 2222.

Euronext.liffe refers to the combined derivatives operations of Euronext and LIFFE, comprising the Euronext derivatives markets in Amsterdam, Brussels, Lisbon, Paris and the LIFFE market in London. This notice is for informational purposes only and does not constitute an offer, solicitation or recommendation to acquire or dispose of any investment or to engage in any other transaction. Those wishing either to trade in any products available on Euronext.liffe's markets or to offer and sell any such products to others should consider both their legal and regulatory position in the relevant jurisdiction and the risks associated with such products before doing so. 4596

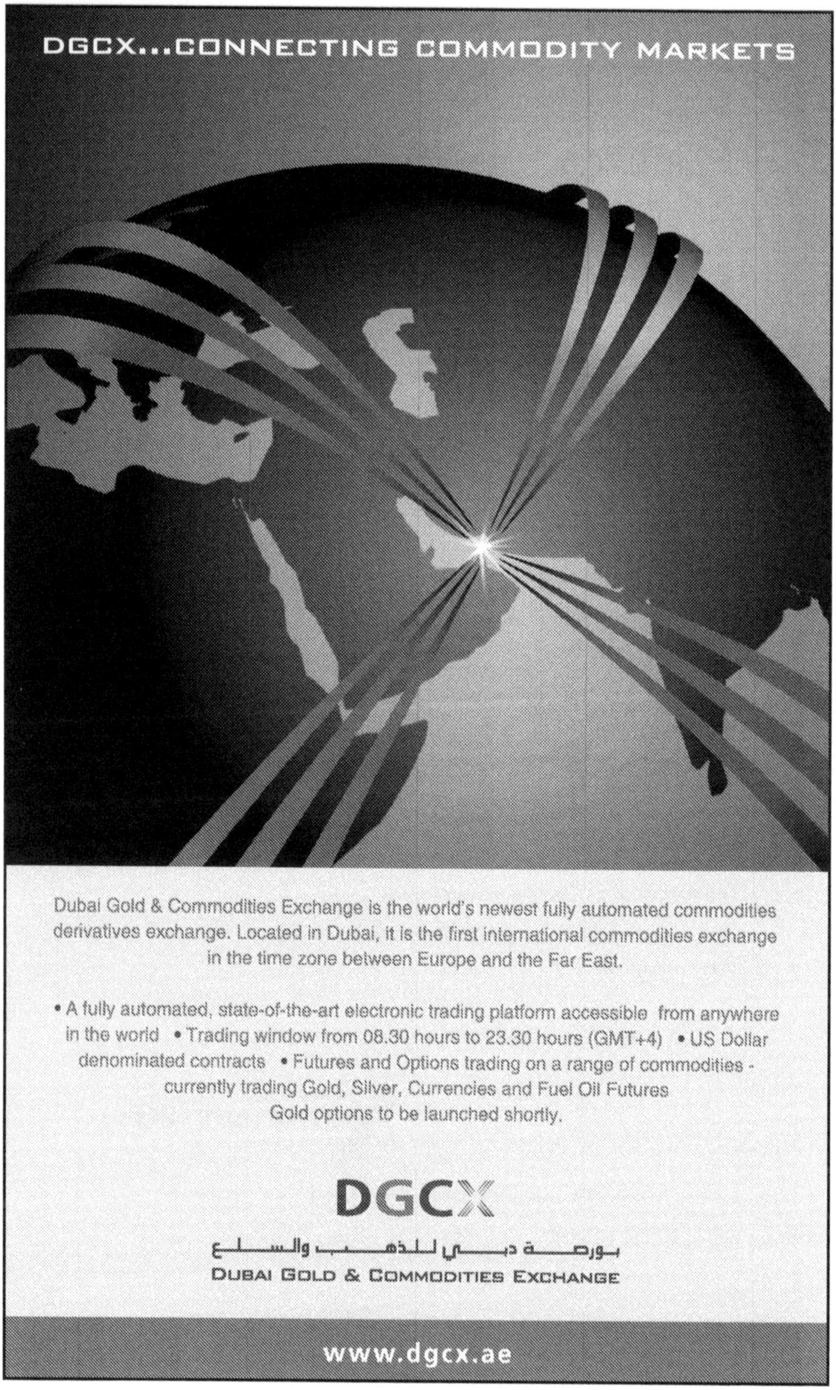
DGCX...CONNECTING COMMODITY MARKETS
Dubai Gold & Commodities Exchange is the world's newest fully automated commodities derivatives exchange. Located in Dubai, it is the first international commodities exchange in the time zone between Europe and the Far East.
• A fully automated, state-of-the-art electronic trading platform accessible from anywhere in the world • Trading window from 08.30 hours to 23.30 hours (GMT+4) • US Dollar denominated contracts • Futures and Options trading on a range of commodities - currently trading Gold, Silver, Currencies and Fuel Oil Futures
Gold options to be launched shortly.
DGCX
بورصة دبي للذهب والسلع
DUBAI GOLD & COMMODITIES EXCHANGE
www.dgcx.ae

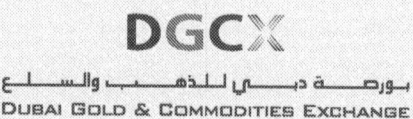

Chapter three

Core Product Concepts: A Simple Primer

The marketplace has made a significant change. The world of derivatives has given way to a marketplace which is truly a derivatives world.

The Exchange Manifesto

"Everything else can wait, but not agriculture."
Pandit Jawaharlal Nehru

The function of the exchange as already outlined is to provide a low cost, low friction environment for trade. The actual markets that an exchange can deal in are many and varied. The only limits are regulation.

At the core of any market is the price of the cash commodity or cash product. This is in other words the cost of the item (often referred to as the underlying) if it was bought right now for delivery at the earliest juncture (note that settlement of many products even "spot" foreign exchange for instance traditionally takes up to 2 days).

Of course, settlement times are a key issue. In the old days of the London Stock Exchange it might be 2 or 3 weeks before stock was delivered and settled. Nowadays most stock exchanges operate on somewhere between T+3 and T+7 (where T stands for "Today").

Ironically, while older legacy markets have tended to struggle to reach rapid settlement, it is usually newer markets which embarrass them. The London based sports exchange Betfair can manage settlement of its sports, political and entertainment futures within 15 minutes of the result of an event being declared (and its number of transactions is vastly higher than the LSE too but that's an aside).

However, not every buyer or seller is looking to purchase a commodity today. Many want to buy for a particular date in the future. For instance a manufacturer who is trying to lock in the price of a particular commodity, say one month in the future, would want a slightly different type of marketplace.

> **Future:**
>
> A future provides the buyer with the obligation to buy the underlying commodity on delivery.
>
> The seller is obliged to deliver the underlying commodity on delivery.

From such demand came the birth of the original "forward" contracts (i.e. a contract you buy now but with delivery some time in the future – forward from the current date).

The modern day future is essentially very similar, except that here contracts are commoditised around a particular settlement month – usually quarterly (most frequently March, June, September and December). In buying a future the purchaser has an obligation to buy the underlying commodity at the price he pays for the future on whatever day is provided as the settlement day. Likewise, a seller of a contract must deliver the appropriate commodity on that day and receive the price the buyer has paid – regardless of what price fluctuations occur in the meantime.

In reality, only a tiny proportion of futures contracts actually reach their expiration and are settled in such a way. Traders and hedgers tend to use the commoditised futures prices to provide them with hedges that they may modify to achieve a hedge more appropriate to their precise needs. Of course, some large hedgers can also skirt round the commoditised exchanges and trade on the OTC market where they can buy a bespoke hedge which precisely meets their needs.

Options contracts are a twist on the futures concept. An option provides the right but not the obligation to buy or sell the underlying marketplace. In this respect, an option is perhaps best thought of in very simple terms as a sort of deposit or an insurance policy. By paying a modest sum of money you can buy a policy (or option) which covers you for a certain outcome. In other words you might be concerned that Gold which is currently at $800 will rise above $1000 before the year's end in a few months time. An appropriate call option can give you the opportunity to insure yourself against such a significant rise. If gold goes up your option profits and you sell it. If gold does not go up, your option expires worthless and you lose the premium you paid for the option.

It falls outside the scope of this book to discuss every single type of derivative or even to delve much deeper into the myriad possibilities available through the use of derivatives. However, it is important to note that there are four core types of participant in all markets:

Brokers: Brokers simply transact business on behalf of other market participants. They are middlemen and have found themselves under increasing threat in the internet age from what is known as disintermediation (the removal of middlemen) thanks to the power of the internet to link buyers and sellers directly.

Hedgers: Hedgers are people who buy or sell derivatives to cover their positions in the underlying marketplace. This may be a mortgage bank which hedges its interest rate exposure and thus can offer a form of interest rate guarantee for the mortgagee. Alternatively, it can be a commodity producer who wants to guarantee a return on his cash crop or livestock while it is still being nurtured. This approach guarantees the producer peace of mind and good cash flow management. It is one reason why derivatives are popular with poorer farmers in India for instance who have woken up to the many advantages provided by the commodity markets there.

Speculators: Traders who have no underlying position to hedge are indulging in price speculation. There is a lot said that is quite unfair about speculators and most of it is also woefully inaccurate. Speculators per se cannot make a market go up or down for any period of time if there is no fundamental reasoning behind a market's strengths/weaknesses. Indeed, the Hunt Brothers (in silver) are just the latest in a very long line of somewhat misguided (and ultimately very bankrupt) individuals who have felt they could "corner" a market and cause it to trade in the direction they wanted it to. Empirical evidence shows that when markets have a reasonable base of liquidity and a choice of derivatives products, it is in fact more difficult to attempt a corner.

A lot of folk like to disparage the art of speculation by claiming that it is just gambling. This is an intriguing response as in fact by the same criteria, all risk is in fact a gamble. This is of course nonsense but then again the fact that a few successful speculators tend to have large fast cars or nice shiny white private jets may also be a reason why they tend to be unpopular amongst those who don't have such accoutrements as personal transport to transport them. In reality, speculators oil the wheels of commerce and help create a marketplace. They are an essential aspect to life – and their risk taking is no more gambling than is any other business decision.

> **Option**
>
> An option provides the buyer with the right (but not the obligation) to buy or sell an underlying commodity (depending on the precise option) on expiry.

Market Makers: Markets need folk to make prices in the very short term – i.e. within the trading day - to ensure that markets can trade smoothly. In this respect, the original commodity markets in the mid West in the 19th century used to encourage those living nearby (the locals) to buy seats (rights to trade) and make prices in the pits to effectively smooth out the friction in the then process between buyers and sellers. As such people effectively created the prices people traded on, they became known as market makers and form a vital function in any exchange. Liquidity is a highly significant component of market success and therefore market makers are keenly encouraged/nurtured by all exchanges, often receiving incentives, such as on their trading and clearing fees especially to support new contracts.

Of course this also raises the issue of broker models and so forth on exchanges. The traditional seat model of exchanges served the purpose of filling floors but nowadays new exchanges are advised not merely to embrace broker intermediation but also to permit direct market access (DMA) for all qualified market participants. This often ruffles feathers with intermediaries but history shows brokers to be just as promiscuous as traders in switching allegiances if an opportunity to profit arises.

When it comes to the brave new world of products, just about everything is currently being added to the pantheon of markets. Traditionally, markets have involved a series of product groups such as the following:

Commodities:

Soft Commodities: Essentially any perishable commodity that is grown, such as wheat and orange juice. Similarly, livestock such as pigs and cows and their related products (some contracts are for live animals some for specific meat cut e.g. pork bellies and so on). Flowers and plants too can be traded in this way with tulips having been part of a form of futures trading as early as the "Tulipomania" in the 1630's.

These markets are likely to grow in breadth and scope in years to come as more and more commodity markets are created for either cash or derivative products.

Energy: Oil and gas have been traded for some years now. However, the concentration has tended to be around the relatively light crude benchmarks such as Brent and West Texas. In other words, the granularity of the market (such as the differently composed crudes from Africa, the Middle East, Eastern Europe and around Borneo) has not generally been represented. However, during 2006 it became clear that several platforms were seeking to list electronic markets that would complement the existing benchmarks and permit separate trading of other oil types and other oil benchmarks. A similar process is likely to occur with gas contracts in due course with fascinating multifaceted ramifications.

The trading of all forms of energy is occurring. Electricity markets have been extant for some years. These products have a series of fascinating trading factors (such as the fact that electricity ultimately is limited in its travelling distance before it biodegrades).

Meanwhile, other fossil fuels such as coal are highly likely to be more widely traded in derivatives products. In fact, any form of harnessable energy power can ultimately be traded – and traded it will likely be!

Finally for those who think energy market hedging is only for the largest multinational energy companies and their largest users such as airlines or multinational transport companies, there is a heart-warming (indeed hearth warming) story of an English central heating oil distributor who a few years ago began selling a form of option allied to his delivery service permitting clients to lock in their future seasonal oil deliveries at the onset of winter.

> **Microtrade**
>
> A Microtrade is a term coined by the author for tiny transactions. This is nowadays recognized as the DNA building block of modern markets. Formerly uneconomic in paper intensive old fashioned floor markets, a Microtrade is now efficient thanks to the increased deployment of Information Technology.

Metals: both precious and more mundane metals from gold and silver to steel and aluminium are already widely traded. The London Metals Exchange has also recently begun trading in Plastics futures. Steel futures markets are only in their infancy.

Emerging Commodity related markets: A whole series of new markets is now emerging in the world of commodities which include the following:

Freight: While some freight markets have been around for some time, the growth in Freight Forwarding Agreements (FFAs) has been considerable in recent years. This market seems likely to continue to grow as more hedging is sought for the increasing trade flows to emerging/from markets such as the BRIC four (Brazil, Russia, India and China).

Water: Various projects have been mooted and a market already exists for water trading in drought-stricken Australia for instance. Indeed, I remain happy to stand by a prediction I made in 1999, that water trading will become one of the largest sources of market activity (the lure of saying liquidity there was considerable but I fought the urge) by 2020.

Equally, while some localised markets in for example rice exist, these are the sorts of agricultural commodities that are going to be traded more frequently as soon as the world's extensive subsidy regimes (or state organised sales operations) are broken down in pertinent commodities. The opportunities for such new commodity products are immense.

Moreover, in an electronic world where just about anything can be traded, the whole notion of what represents an asset class is shifting. The traditional bankers' view of property or hardware/machinery as being just about the only items worth securing a loan against is therefore likely to crumble in due course.

In the world of the fascinatingly intangible, there are some tantalising areas of product growth taking place at the moment.

Weather: The weather is increasingly proving a focus of interest to the derivatives world. This ought to be received joyously by businesses of every hue – and not just the agriculturalists. For restaurant and café owners, products already exist OTC which provide a return in the event that weather is insufficiently clement to permit practicable use of a terrace in summer for instance.

Emissions: These are the second link in this exotic new world of products which are in some ways linked to weather regardless of where you sit in the cyclical/global warming debate over climate change. Exchanges devoted to emissions trading have already been born in Chicago and Europe amongst other regions with the mandate to facilitate the free trading of permits. As the movement to find a more harmonious balance in Planet Earth's environment continues, the prospects for carbon trading and related emissions markets look very promising – especially as outmoded concepts of subsidy are simply going to be impossible for governments to finance as the baby boomer generation's retirement squeezes future revenues.

Financial derivatives: Products are based around several simple premises:

Deposits: simple 3-month deposit futures and options contracts abound in sophisticated economies, whether it is for the British Sterling Market, the Eurozone or the US dollar deposit market. All such products and their many related OTC brethren (such as FRAs and swaps and so on) create massive hedging opportunities for governments, corporates and even individuals to hedge their bond/loan/mortgage interest rate. Moreover, in the cash exchange business, online markets such as Zopa are now threatening to revolutionise simple cash lending through their provision of a bank which effectively acts as an exchange matching lenders and borrowers.

Foreign Exchange: Naturally, foreign exchange is a rich resource for traded markets. When the Bretton Woods agreement broke down in August 1971, the start of the modern deregulatory wave began and competition became a great deal more marked between different economies. Foreign exchange futures were the first financial futures products and they were in the vanguard as financial deregulation under President Nixon began to change the global financial marketplace. The one clear issue is that any nation with a form of capital or foreign exchange movement restriction suffers against those markets which are more open. Certainly developing an internationally oriented exchange with such prohibitions on capital in force is not sensible.

Bonds: While mortgage backed bonds were the initial futures contracts in this segment, it was in Government Bond futures that the derivatives market has made a highly significant impact, permitting governments and even corporate bond issuers to hedge their issues in the marketplace. The end result (as with cash deposit markets) has made the government bond market significantly more liquid and transparent than ever before.

Wherever financial products expand, whether it be in new nations or currency zones or in new products themselves, such as credit derivatives (which provide coverage against a default by a particular company/issuer), once again the possibilities are simply immense.

For those who are sceptical that financial derivatives are feasible in their country, a useful tale is that of the London International Financial Futures Exchange (LIFFE). Before trading began in 1982, the exchange was concerned about scepticism amongst the major inter-bank dealers that in fact the cash 3 month deposit market was not liquid enough to support a futures market.

Equities: The equity derivatives market was initially driven by the USA where modern financial futures and options products were developed. However, the fact that financial and commodity futures & options are regulated by the CFTC and equities and related products are predominantly regulated by the SEC did not help the USA maintain its lead in product development. While US volume remains huge, much of the most innovative activity in equity derivatives in recent years has come from Asia and Europe.

Stock Options: The original equity derivatives were traded options (as opposed to options granted by a company to staff for productivity and so on) and have been trading since 1973 at the Chicago Board Options Exchange. Nowadays they are offered world wide on a vast array of exchanges, based upon many thousands of underlying equities. Options have also metarmophosed to provide more bespoke possibilities on many exchanges. In recent years the London-based Euronext.LIFFE derivatives market has been pioneering some interesting ways of melding together OTC and exchange traded equity products. The possibilities for stock options are enormous and restricted only by the number of liquid underlying shares – of which there remain thousands at the time of writing - which could support options.

Stock Indices: Are available as futures, options, Exchange Traded Funds and various other forms. Initially these were based on very broad indices such as the American Value Line, S&P 100 and S&P 500 indices. Nowadays, having a national stock index is a sort of economic virility test amongst governments it seems (like having a national bourse and futures exchange or a national airline). Fortunately, the provision of a national index can remain while the prospect of maintaining national exchanges may not be the best idea when faced with more efficient regional structures for providing exchanges.

At any rate, the whole business of indexing particular sectors (including commodities and non-equity products) is massive and will continue to grow exponentially. Increasing numbers of sectoral indices being listed and the growth in cross border trading means that more international indices are created in years to come – regardless of whether the actual cash exchanges come together through merger and acquisition.

Single Stock Futures: Actually a reinvention pioneered in recent years by exchanges such as Hong Kong and also this author, the Single Stock Future was stunted at re-birth in the USA through the regulatory turf war of the CFTC and SEC. SSFs themselves have a history dating back to the Amsterdam Bourse several hundred years ago when clear antecedents were being traded. Once again the future for single stock futures is very bright although interestingly their growth to date has often been beyond the major markets of Europe or USA. Rather, Single Stock Futures have proven very popular in markets such as India and Russia where there have been difficulties in making delivery of cash stock work smoothly. Therefore, futures have taken their place and become very popular instruments for gaining exposure to a share price.

The Next Dimension: Product development is also expanding into areas which established exchanges have previously flirted with but never actually established products upon. This is remarkable as in fact I firmly believe the largest traded segment within 25 years will be products based upon sports and entertainment. The London-based exchange Betfair for instance leads the field in the business of sports and event markets. With 150,000 regular users matching 5,000,000 trades per day, in something like 4000 active markets, the exchange has a simply remarkable order flow – and all of it comes direct to the exchange. Betfair is the 500lb gorilla of the sports and entertainment market nowadays but the market has simply incredible expansion opportunity. The popularity of all forms of sports and entertainments as well as politics, are well known the world over and yet the possibilities of that marketplace are quite simply unquantifiable.

Thanks to electronic infrastructure, the future of product development is bounded only by the limits of human ingenuity. This is truly a golden age of product development and as such the opportunities are everywhere.

NEW YORK BOARD OF TRADE

Since 1870, New York's Original Futures Exchange
A Tradition of Innovation

Where the world trades the things you use everyday

...Cocoa... Coffee... Cotton... USDX...
OJ... Pulp... Sugar... Currencies...

Learn more about us
www.nybot.com - www.nybotlive.com
1-800-HEDGE-IT

The Exchange Manifesto

Spice up your portfolio –

Options on Euro-Schatz, Euro-Bobl, Euro-Bund Futures

Flavor your trading with Eurex options on fixed income futures: Looking to add the strength of Euro-Schatz, -Bobl or -Bund Futures to your asset allocation while retaining liquidity? Options on fixed income derivatives at Eurex are your best choice. Whether enhancing or protecting the performance of Euro government bond portfolios, options on debt futures at Eurex give your investments that extra flavor. Wishing you an abundant business! www.eurexchange.com

Chapter four

Infrastructure and the Requirements & Technology to Create a Market

Electronic exchange markets are simply the cheapest means of facilitating commerce anywhere in the world. Equally they can provide a range of benefits to a greater diaspora of citizens and corporations than any other transactional method.

The Exchange Manifesto

"Platforms – the basic underlying operating systems for innovation and production – do not change very often."

Thomas Friedman

All exchange operators require three vital functions to ensure an orderly market which is customer-centric in the contemporary age:

>Technology
>Technology
>Technology

It would be a severe understatement to say that the modern exchange is based upon a strong technological infrastructure. Rather, without a strong technological structure, the exchange is little more than a form of sophisticated board game as opposed to a pivotal vehicle for promoting and propagating commerce.

The most encouraging news is that thanks to the vast developments of the first internet decade, exchange technology infrastructure need not be absurdly expensive. Naturally, a large internationally networked exchange such as EUREX, the leading European derivatives marketplace with operations stretching world wide, needs a remarkably extensive server infrastructure and a huge dedicated network to ensure ultra rapid performance. However, smaller markets only require a very modest amount of technological infrastructure. It is feasible to create an exchange nowadays with a total budget below 1 million dollars and indeed some exchanges have been established for significantly less.

Just like an automobile, those who are seeking to have a very fast vehicle which traverses all known terrain, or which is designed for its own race circuit will cost a great deal more than a family runabout saloon. Exchanges ought to be adopting technology which best fits their likely volume. Unfortunately a great many men (and it is invariably men) harbour desires to have technology that vastly overperforms what they require. Often the situation is a sort of "server envy" to borrow from Freudian logic: because one nearby exchange has a considerable technology infrastructure from a major brand provider, so too they must buy a similar system. Similarly, neighbours the world over compete to buy BMWs and Mercedes while they will rarely benefit from a great deal of the utility of their luxury brands on 'the school run'. Then again, if neighbours are spending their own hard earned cash then it's nobody else's business. The issue with exchanges is that here shareholder funds are being deployed and this author is a strong advocate of buying a small system up front with the option to scale up where required. Exchanges can always adopt new technology as they grow.

Building versus buying is another issue. In the past, the issues were more clear cut. The likes of the LIFFE exchange in London for instance built their own system as they felt uncomfortable buying other systems which were then operated by the software arms of competitor exchanges. True, most exchange technology and certainly the IT for basic markets can be built very easily these days. That said, it seems to be counterproductive as, in the modern age, almost every possible level of IT infrastructure is available to the end user from small market solutions such as those provided by the likes of COMDAQ through to the larger systems provided by companies such as Deutsche Börse systems and the OM technology which is operated by more exchanges world-wide than any other system. Equally, it can often be much simpler and more cost effective to maintain "off the shelf" software as opposed to home built packages. There are a myriad of vendors who can produce solutions for all manner of markets.

Nevertheless, regardless of budget, the necessary precepts are the same. It falls outside the scope of this brief tome to outline the precise technologies that can be deployed but the core concepts are the same. The bare necessities of the technology required for an exchange are as follows (my thanks to Colin Howard, Chairman of COMDAQ for his input to this section):

Preliminaries: A new exchange will require a suitable trading network. Major markets such as CME, Deutsche Börse, Euronext and NASDAQ have either built their own or rely heavily on existing vast networks such as those provided by Equant (itself originally the network of the world's air traffic controllers). That said, the majority of smaller markets and all the microexchanges I can think of utilise that wonderful, ubiquitous wide area network (WAN) the, World Wide Web (WWW), or internet.

1) A matching engine: There needs to be a core facility where all trades are actually executed. This matching engine is the heart of the trading system. It need not be very complex and many exchanges seem driven to provide matching engines which can transact vast multiples of trades per second. In reality, such high speed processing is only required by a tiny minority of exchange applications. Nevertheless, a matching engine must be flexible and ought to be clearly scoped by the exchange operators in negotiation with their software supplier. The extent of negotiability built into a trading engine is of course a key element both for the matching engine itself and also the front end trading system (see point 2 below) by which users will actually seek to transact their business. Finally, the matching engine is a vital facility as once it has matched a trade, the engine must then generate via the database the necessary contracts for eventual settlement of a position which also creates a (trackable) logistics chain.

2) A front end: The GUI (Graphical User Interface) is the core frontal interface by which brokers and traders will access the market. This may be a very simple order entry screen or it may have the capacity to suggest a series of different parameters for particular trades which therefore leads to a requirement for this GUI to incorporate the necessary screens to allow for negotiation between counterparties.

3) Messaging: Particularly where some element of negotiation is involved, the system ought to also include a messaging system to permit a free flow of information which is secure, encrypted and virus free thus encouraging dialogue for those who are the closed user group of the community.

4) Database: A multi-functional database which lists and has the appropriate trading permissions and membership criteria of all traders and their companies is essential to the operation of all other components of the exchange as well as of course being the core database of records holding the details of the trades entered (including orders cancelled and so on) and executed.

5) Administration: Separate from the database per se, the system must have appropriate administrative support tools to allow exchange users to manage their own data (passwords, contact details, delivery addresses and so on).

6) Clearing/Finance & Payments: The more commoditised markets will utilise immediate clearing systems through a clearing house structure. Other markets, usually in some form of physical commodity will deploy a myriad of potential financing solutions whether it is a form of escrow or some other linkage to trade finance/electronic letters of credit and so on.

Ultimately, to complete any transaction, the IT requires an integrated payments and reporting structure which monitors the compliance of agreements relating to the agreed contract.

7) Settlement & Delivery: In addition to the payments side of the trade (point 6), the IT system will require (particularly where any physical settlement is necessary), databases holding details warranting the certified identity, quality/condition and specified location of deliverable commodities. To assist with the process of settlement, linkage to transportation at the lowest cost for moving settled goods (by whatever means) is an essential factor in easing the settlement and delivery process.

8) Risk Management: Usually this will involve both an element of pre-emptive risk management where the exchange (and/or its intermediaries) pre-screen trades before execution in an effort to ensure that traders do not over-reach their credit limits and so on. Post trade, the exchange needs to ensure that whatever payments (whether direct to delivery or margining) are required for the market to function in an orderly fashion, the exchange and its clearing systems are not subject to any risk beyond that necessary to create the transaction itself.

9) Surveillance/Compliance: Some might well argue compliance /surveillance comes first but with recourse to the chicken/egg dichotomy, it strikes me as best to build an exchange first, then oversee it. Nevertheless creating functioning surveillance/compliance is vital at all stages. Without compliance functionality a market can operate. However, the market's integrity can easily be called into question. To that end, the market requires a surveillance function whereby certain (exchange employed) parties (independent of the trading infrastructure) can oversee the activity in the market and monitor for behaviour that is contrary to the rules of the exchange and which may cause financial losses or other activity that may bring the exchange into disrepute. Moreover, the IT infrastructure ought to include (see also point 3) a clear means by which disputes and other problems can be resolved rapidly. Market confidence is remarkably fragile. Many exchanges have discovered this to their cost in the past. Most larger exchanges tend to operate with at least two full trading systems for maximum redundancy in their exchange hub. Often one is used for training and education purposes in real time. Note however that it is not unknown for exchange staff to make basic errors in this regard. In the case of one leading derivatives exchange, an IT staffer inadvertently powered down the live market erroneously thinking it was the back-up server. The problem was compounded by the fact that rebooting the system took over 20 mintues, which felt like an eternity to the real-time interest rate and equity futures/options traders using that exchange.

Disaster Recovery
A vital issue for the efficient operation of an exchange is to have a suitable disaster recovery plan and preferably a separate disaster recovery site ought to be deployed.

The core precepts of disaster recovery, requiring separation but proximity of backup office, a comprehensive plan for evacuation and opening of the disaster recovery site have been written up by many other consultants and IT experts, so I won't dwell upon them here.

Website
The final, vital prerequisite for any exchange is its website. In this respect, a vast amount of the public image and branding of the exchange will frequently be encountered via the website.

Therefore, the site needs to be soundly designed (alas an all too irregular event on the internet these days) and coded in a fashion that takes into account the likely bandwidth of the main users.

In terms of information, the website will be a key interface for describing and updating to potential traders all about the business of the exchange. Moreover, a key issue ought to be to endeavour to facilitate the signing up of new market participants.

The Exchange Manifesto

Registration ought to be simple to effect through the exchange as well as permitting existing users to change their details and so forth.

Moreover, details of any exchange initiatives, new products and so on ought to be provided via the exchange. There are various simple online databases to facilitate exchange news, including all exchange notices, member/trader/product announcements etc such as www.bourseinformation.com.

The website can also be deployed for online educational activities. A full trading demo ought to be available, to permit potential participants to gain experience in how the marketplace works.

The vital importance of a website is in providing the major front window for exchanges in an electronic age (where large city centre buildings with floors no longer advertise the existence of an exchange presence). After all, what every exchange needs to thrive upon is a community. By melding a community of interested parties to trade on your market, the ultimate result is a better marketplace. No exchange operator can ever afford to lose sight of the community he must meld.

Operation of an Exchange
Operation of the exchange follows logically on from the IT infrastructure. Naturally, no single general outline tome can hope to discuss in detail what is required to run an exchange in its entirety but as a guide, the following are the key functions required.

Of course a usual structure like any corporate entity with a Chairman (who may be executive or non-executive) and a CEO management etc. is a given, although the precise size must be kept to a minimum in such a commoditised business.

Moreover, in the modern age, the vast majority of exchanges are now for-profit entities. Those who have a desire for a co-operative structure can of course found a mutual but the vogue nowadays tends to be almost inevitably towards for-profit structure.

In either case, an exchange needs to decide upon a structure for its traders. Even many for-profit exchanges with mutual origins still refer to "members" although those members do not have to be shareholders as such (or at least are certainly not the only shareholders). Some trading rights are only granted with a certain quantity of shares being held by the "member" company. However, for a start up exchange, it is advisable to concentrate initially on building the trading community rather than being concerned with the concept of underpinning a share price.

Originally exchanges had a limited number of trading permits or "seats" which were generally regulated by the amount of space on the floor to access a particular market. However, such permits have tended to prove unwieldy in many respects and can often result in certain products' growth being stunted by seat-holders preferring other products and so on. In fact the simplest way of all to guarantee simple access to markets is to make trading access free. Those intermediaries who wish to use a market also ought to be permitted free access. Nowadays, most smaller new markets tend to provide free trading access through the internet to traders with modest fee structures (cost plus a modest margin pricing basis) in the event of a market user requiring direct access through a specific network (as opposed to the internet).

The business of an exchange ought to be making a return on the transactions it oversees and to this end, the bulk of income will come from trading and clearing fees. Generally very modest micropayments compared to transaction values are the order of the day.

Naturally, therefore markets need an efficient operating structure. This can be effected in various ways but it tends to help if one particular person is given the role of actually ensuring the day-to-day operation of an exchange. This may be the Market Secretary or an Operations Director. This person must have the complete power to open and close markets in the event of force majeure (e.g. in the wake of a major disruption to telephone services, or banking whether through natural disaster or other event e.g. terrorism and so on).

In this respect, no exchange is complete without a rule book. Rule books tend to grow with experience and indeed they are invariably fairly comprehensive undertakings. Auction rules and so forth need to be discussed and outlined, along with order entry procedures, market conduct rules, arbitration issues, clearing and settlement procedures and so forth. All data relating to market changes, opening hours (e.g. for holidays) need to be issued through the Market Secretary or an equivalent office.

Ensuring compliance with these rules is the responsibility of the Market Surveillance department which as noted above must have a capacity for total access to all aspects of the IT system to ensure that rules are being adhered to.

Naturally, like all companies, marketing is a key aspect to the business as is the PR function. In many respects, PR is one of the most vital issues facing markets today. It lines up directly with the education issue and cannot be underestimated. The media can understandably find the practice of what often appear to be arcane exchange markets, somewhat difficult to grasp. The exchange will need to concentrate on ensuring that its messages are clear when it comes to the practical benefits for all aspects of an exchange market. The simple truth is that markets bring liquidity and transparency to the transactional process. Nevertheless, the processes need to be made clear to all parties as the process can often be difficult to follow for the media. Thus in many respects the jobs of PR and the educational department will often move in tandem, particularly at the start of the exchange where it cannot be underestimated just how much effort needs to be placed in making the processes and benefits of the market understood by politicians, government and all other interested parties. Moreover, often exchanges will be unpopular with existing vested-interest groups (usually intermediaries) who see little benefit to their existing businesses being disintermediated or at least marginal returns squeezed.

Note that when it comes to market education and quite frequently PR too, nothing beats good old fashioned face-to-face meetings and leg work. Educational seminars for example can be of benefit online in a "webinar" format but despite the wondrous advantages of new technology, it is truly the personal touch which tends to make the biggest impact.

One excellent example of the benefits of face-to-face marketing on the road comes from the educational experiences of Rod Gravelet-Blondin, the man behind the remarkable rise in the South African Futures Exchange's (SAFEX) agricultural commodity division (SAFEX has since become an integral part of the Johannesburg Stock Exchange). He was faced with the job of educating South Africa's farmers about the benefits of the new derivatives products which would provide hedging opportunities in place of the comparatively expensive government maize board and other bodies.

So, Rod took to the road and used local farmers as a central organiser of an event to educate. The Farmers would convene in a barn somebody was appointed to bring drinks and food (usually a cow), while others would provide the wood and so forth to create a barbecue to cook. Rod would discuss the basics of futures (once the farmers had been politely asked to disarm and leave their arsenal of weapons in safe hands at the door) and afterwards socialise with the farmers, answering their questions over a beverage and some splendidly barbecued beef. Such marketing required a lot of mileage around South Africa but it paid dividends – the SAFEX division of JSE remains one of the most successful agricultural markets in the world despite being barely a decade old.

The Exchange Manifesto

JSE Limited
Agricultural Products Division
Private Bag X991174,
Sandton, 2146
South Africa
Tel: 27 (011) 520 7535

Successful agriculture is all about using resources productively and managing risks effectively. No one can afford not to manage the price risk in South African agriculture.

Chapter five

Clearing & Confidence: The Great Imperative

The most significant issue for global financial markets remains the fact that the finance industry can provide elegant solutions to many problems, thus enhancing the business of commerce, providing government co-operates with a suitably elegant regulatory structure. This is a win-win which no government can afford to ignore.

The Exchange Manifesto

"Like fire, the gift of Prometheus to humanity, full capital movement can either benefit the world or harm it. Fire has the potential to provide warmth and light, but it can also cause death and destruction.

The movement towards full capital mobility likewise has the potential to benefit all of us. It has the power to unleash a wave of global capitalism that will provide prosperity to the world's citizens. But, if the governments of the world misstep, it has the potential to create financial instability that could devastate the world's economy."

Lowell Bryan and Dana Farrell

The reason why people decide to either leave their money under the mattress or to deposit it with the bank is usually dictated by safety. Without a financial system where the public are confident, the financial system itself cannot exist in any cohesive form for the good of society. In the modern era confidence in the system is of particular importance as the "fiat" money system means that cash itself no longer has any direct relationship to a significant underlying – such as gold or a similar precious metal. To this end, the major currencies such as the Euro or the Dollar are measured by a sort of very vague indicative feeling of how particular currency zones are performing, their relative economic stability, flexibility and growth and so on. For smaller currencies, it can be very difficult to engender confidence but it is equally a great deal easier to see confidence disintegrate in a small currency.

Governments, alas, often find markets a nauseating irritant. It is a pity that they cannot seem to follow that markets are ultimately right and as English Parliamentarian Enoch Powell famously noted "all political careers ultimately end in failure." French finance ministers, for instance, at any point when their economy is under pressure, are wont to complain about currency speculators or others selling against the "best" interests of the French government. They denounce pragmatic traders as "agiteurs" and demand their execution (as was the fashion during Revolutionary times). Ironically, such rhetoric only highlights both the relative powerlessness of the politicians and the fact that markets do hold the trump card – sheer size. As President Clinton's election strategist James Carville memorably remarked: when he died, he wanted to be reincarnated as the Bond Market, as that way he could bully everybody in a way that elected US Presidents could only dream of!

Politicians who tweak their policies to be market friendly can enjoy great benefits. Markets, while deemed fickle, are in fact only seeking to make returns in a manner which provides the least resistance.

An exchange marketplace simply cannot function if it is seen as an extension of the government or some major interest group. Without confidence in a nation, the exchange and local market is simply not going to function.

To that end, avoiding the mistakes made by other governments ought not to be very difficult. However, as the Thai government demonstrated in late 2006, reading financial history is evidently not common, at least not amongst governments created by coups anyway. The Thai government tried in a ham-fisted way to limit speculative flows into the economy, and imposed restrictions on foreign capital entering the country. Foreign capital promptly exited stage left and the Thais were forced into an embarrassing volte-face within hours.

Nevertheless, the damage will remain for some time and the Thai government has demonstrated itself as being ignorant of markets. In this competitive world where foreign direct investment agencies from throughout the world are often engaged in cut throat competition, no nation on earth can afford to impede the free-flowing wheels of capitalism when there is a competitor (usually just across the neighbouring frontier) ready to profit from its slip-ups. Moreover, it ought to be noted that it is not just emerging market governments such as the Thais who can create legislation that is anti-market. The USA saw a political bandwagon gain steam against corporate corruption in the wake of the Enron fiasco. While the origins of the political concern were entirely understandable, the resultant legislation was made in haste and as such was not the most brilliant of solutions. With corporate compliance costs soaring, US exchanges have been suffering widespread delisting by overseas companies with business being gained by other financial centres, most notably London, whose stock exchange has become the overseas listing venue of choice for companies in rapidly growing major populous nations such as China, India and Russia. The US will presumably win business back in due course when it waters down the regulatory excesses of the Sarbanes Oxley legislation. That said, never let it be forgotten that America's withholding tax impositions of the 1960s effectively kick-started the process of changing the postwar, post-colonial and relatively sleepy City of London into the financial powerhouse it is today.

Withholding taxes can be popular with unenlightened governments as they appear to be a "painless" method of raising taxes. Invariably, they involve considerable commercial risks. The German government of Chancellor Kohl had to rescind legislation on a withholding tax for government bonds due to an immediate outflux of bond investment from that country. Ironically, had the Germans paid attention to similar issues in Sweden some years earlier, they would have learnt that in an electronic marketplace, the daftest of government regulation (or even apparently sensible legislation that just creates irritating bureaucracy and frictional cost) is in danger of being entirely avoided through the rerouting of electronic orders.

The OM exchange famously provided a brilliant solution to a Swedish government imposition of withholding tax on bonds. It created a London exchange using the same OM technology but safely domiciled outside Scandinavia. Dealers were given the choice of executing their orders in high-tax Sweden or low-tax London. Remarkably, the business flowed straight out of Stockholm and the Swedish government was forced to rescind its erroneous law.

So, no nation can truly afford to impose too much on the marketplace nor can they afford to rest on their laurels in anticipation of a "just distribution" of investment funds. True, the precise metrics of what investors are likely to risk will also vary according to country and thus some larger resource rich nations may be able to tweak the rules a little more aggressively than their smaller competitors for instance but ultimately no nation is immune to an investor strike if it opts for the wrong regulatory mix.

The Exchange Manifesto

With the right regulatory mix of course, confidence can grow, and markets flourish. Nevertheless, the whole fragile issue of trust needs to include a sound banking system which people have faith in. To that end, the most basic of economies need to find a way to engender confidence in people not to keep their money under the mattress but to place it in banks and thus create loans which help to oil the wheels of commerce.

With a banking system comes a clearing system (the method of offsetting different bank transactions against each other) which itself needs to be sufficiently robust to ensure confidence in the system both locally and internationally.

Allied to the banking clearing system and a vital part of the exchange process itself is the clearing house (and settlements depositary). This is relevent for all exchange-related transactions whether in commodities, or financial products, or equity, or any other product segment.

The clearing house is commonly known as the central counter-party. In other words when a transaction is created, the clearing house effectively intermediates in the executed trade and guarantees the transaction between the two transaction participants (counterparties).

Of course, the counterparties themselves are expected to be in good standing with the clearing house (and brokers must do their utmost to ensure that they have sufficient understanding of their clients, preferably sufficient collateral on account, to undertake their positions). Nevertheless, unfortunate circumstances do arise and this is where clearing houses become vital. The venerable, if accident prone, Barings Bank collapsed in February 1995 due to the fraudulent trading activities of Nick Leeson going unnoticed by evidently inefficient management. The fact that the clearing houses in London, Singapore and other world markets had highly significant reserves meant that the crisis was rapidly dissipated before it became a financial panic. Central Banks and regulators have of course a key role to play in endeavouring to dissipate such panics but the strength of the clearing house will remain paramount in the minds of investors.

Traditionally clearing houses in the derivatives markets have levied "margins" against positions, a form of working deposit.

This is highly capital-efficient for investors/traders/hedgers, banks and so on, but of course the element of what margin is the most judicious to match market efficiency is one which is highly prized amongst the skills set of clearing house managers. Margins are set at an initial rate (usually a flat cash sum representing a certain percentage of the underlying contract value) while the positions themselves are daily (at least) marked to market by the clearing house to ensure that any losing position is covered by the party which is losing money. Moreover, clearing systems operate to provide the most efficient use of capital and thus provide special margin rates for "offsetting" positions, where risk is reduced thanks to related "legs" and so on. Achieving balance on a clearing system over margins is very important as usually the alternative is for transactions to be undertaken on the OTC market where the clearing system is not so clean-cut. Large banks and similar counterparties feel comfortable managing their risks bilaterally but central banks, regulators and so forth tend to prefer encouraging business on exchange. Moreover, a thriving exchange market (thanks to competitive margining) not only represents an ultimately more secure financial system in many regards, it also permits smaller players to access the market at the wholesale rates which they may not be able to remotely achieve if they have to deal on credit with only their balance sheet as collateral. Indeed, it is notable that cash foreign exchange dealing amongst every institution below very large banks down to the smallest individual hedgers/speculators has now begun to take place on a margined trading basis Margining needs to be sensible to preclude business going OTC but the better a clearing house can organise margins to encourage exchange trading, the more beneficial the results will be for all participants. Note of course that higher margins tend to be imposed in practice by brokers on their smallest clients anyway as a means of reducing the brokers risk exposure.

Clearing the finances of trades also leads to settlement and here again the vital issue must be the efficient management of the different client positions. Settlement depositaries for bonds and equities for instance tend to hold a great deal of client information and data – nowadays increasingly in electronic (as opposed to paper) form. This naturally helps with the process of regulating and organising markets, reducing money laundering by bearer bond holders for example as well as providing for an orderly transition in the sale of positions to other parties. Moreover, commodity clearing houses must undertake the organisation of delivery systems (in conjunction with the exchanges) to ensure that particular commodities delivered to the required locale are of the agreed quality/quantity and so on.

Of course, the commoditisation of products is vital here. The individual characteristics of sheep for instance makes wool notoriously difficult to commoditise, which is probably why creating exchange markets has been a problem. Gold, silver or other precious metals on the other hand are fairly simple to grade by quality/purity and thus have thriving cash, forward and derivatives markets.

That clearing houses require confidence in their ability to operate cannot be emphasised enough. However, they also need two other key factors, a very good balance sheet (and hence a high credit rating – the top grade "AAA" is preferred) and a very considerable rule book which effectively allows for a process to deal with every possible eventuality in the marketplace.

In terms of technology, the processing required by a clearing house – while considerable and complex – is not that difficult to resource. The major clearing systems for payments and also financial market transactions have tended to create their own processes but equally there are ways to fast-track the system creation to build new clearing houses if they are required. For instance, the existing networks of telecoms companies (fixed line or mobile) are effectively brilliant clearing systems. The nature of a clearing system is that it requires confidential billing, with many low cost but high value transactions. Telephone companies already compare networks that involve a vast amount of real-time processing with the capacity to bill many small transactions easily and reliably. Ironically when first presented with this opportunity, many telephone companies shied away from the opportunity to create such new clearing systems, preferring instead to spend their money on 3G networks. Ah, the joys of 20:20 hindsight...

Separating Clearing and Settlement
A great deal of argument has ensued in different nations about the separation of clearing/settlement with the front end exchange systems. This often heated debate has effectively failed to create a simple solution – so the argument will likely rage for some years

to come.

In the USA, the futures & options exchanges have traditionally operated with an integral clearing house (a unique exception being the Chicago Board of Trade which divorced its near relative operation The Cleaning Corp (née BOTCC) and subsequently saw clearing subsumed into the Chicago Mercantile Exchange. Integrated operations such as CME are known as "vertical silos" as a result of their capacity to create a straight through process within the same exchange from execution to clearing/settlement.

Equity clearing has in the USA been created around a single clearing utility, the Depositary Trust & Clearing Corporation while equity options utilise the Options Clearing Corporation. Bonds similarly clear through the Government Securities Clearing Corporation. While many academic studies exist, it is simply not clear that these utilities do reduce clearing costs or aid the clearing process in a complex hybrid asset market. After all a hybrid derivatives/cash market position in US traded entities requires processing across several clearing houses with little offset between them. In Europe, the clearing houses are mixed. Several silos exist such as Deutsche Börse which is particularly unpopular with many, especially in the UK. Alas, the London Stock Exchange which has remained one of the world's greatest markets despite fairly woeful management of many projects in the post war era, became separated from its own settlement process due to the sheer inability of the then stock exchange management to actually create a viable electronic processing network. One lives in hope the same team are not involved with London's Olympic preparations for 2012, although naturally one may see their hands in the construction of the much-delayed new Wembley national soccer stadium.

That said, London remains a core epicentre of the financial markets and its largest international financial centre with some very strong clearing and settlement processes. Perhaps ironically, while there is significant confidence in the banking system (i.e. little fear of banks going bust) the actual process of banking in the UK remains an utterly third world experience. Thankfully, the concentrated incompetence within the UK banking system has not (at any rate not yet) sapped confidence in the UK clearing system for financial markets although it must be a matter for concern.

So, there are those in Europe who look to the USA and claim that they are being charged excessive fees for clearing and often seek to have some form of utility for the entire European market imposed. It is not within the scope of this tome to discuss all the issues. Nevertheless, one is inclined to wonder just how a non-competitive utility can be deemed the most successful means to organise capitalism – particularly a single silo where little or no cross asset margining is available. Clearly, there is no distinct model preferred by all players and while a voluble few have made many utterances on the issue, nevertheless, the European issues are somewhat different to those faced by many other nations whether developing, or small, or both.

Bilateral clearing and the use of guarantees cannot be discounted in an effort to get simple trading systems up and running. The key issue above all remains one of instilling confidence in the system itself. Many small commodity markets have deployed different forms of escrow to try and produce a system of clearing to assist in the process of building a market. Another sensible innovation, promoted by Kevin Potter, founder of Sandbox Technologies in South Africa is to utilise an Electronic Warehouse Receipt (EWR) which has been certified by the warehouse operator as essentially a tradable instrument in its own right. The possibilities for clearing to develop are considerable, based around those core precepts of financial probity, integrity and trust, married to a strong legal system where property laws and the opportunity to enforce debts are respected.

Moreover, we cannot avoid the issue that the "DNA" of financial life is what I christened the "microtrade" and that the process of building trade in many markets must begin from a very low base level.

Mohammed Yunus, through his work with Grameen Bank, has become the most famous exponent of the Microbanking revolution. While microbanking has brought hope and prosperity to millions of people throughout the world's poorest regions, the fact that electronic trading can now provide similar microtrading opportunities in all manner of marketplaces beyond traditional borrowing and lending means that the opportunity to expand the process of commercially growing prosperity can reach a vast number more people in just about any form of commerce the world over.

Naturally, a clearing system must be managed in a way to ensure that money laundering is not an issue. However, equally, this raises other significant issues. For instance, a group of rural farmers in East Africa may be unable to access hedging opportunities through agricultural markets in the established worlds as they fundamentally fail basic anti-money laundering documentation (such as passports or utility bills). Various attempts have been made in recent years by international bodies to ameliorate such impasses. When farmers are able to hedge it gives them a materially better chance of sustainable economic advancement.

Under the auspices of the World Bank and UNCTAD, hedging programmes have been used in several developing nations. These provide easier access to established markets for co-operatives or other groups of farmers who otherwise lack the required developed world paperwork to pass money laundering and Know Your Client ("KYC") tests. Increasingly such programmes can be tailored to, and indeed exploit the advantages of, more local marketplaces for the hedging process in the electronic age.

Naturally, clear rule of law and a sound financial system are vital aspects to clearing, but it can never be forgotten that the whole issue of confidence remains a very precious aspect of financial markets – and particularly their clearing systems.

The Exchange Manifesto

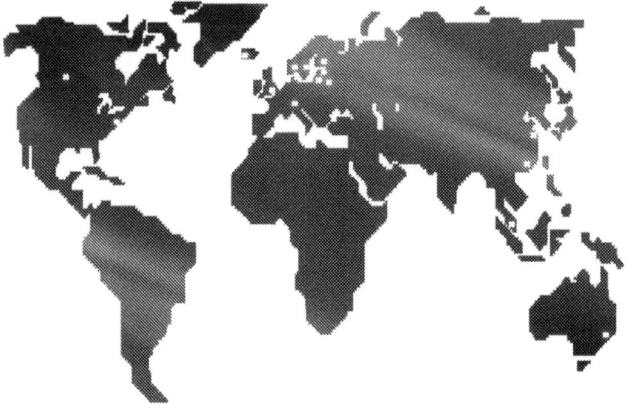

OMX is a leading expert in the exchange industry. Through the Nordic Exchange in Copenhagen, Stockholm, Helsinki, Riga, Tallinn and Vilnius, OMX offers access to approximately 80 percent of the Nordic and Baltic securities market. Our integrated technology solutions span the transaction chain enabling efficient securities transactions. With more than 60 customers in over 50 countries, OMX is the world's foremost provider of marketplace solutions for exchanges, clearing organizations and central securities depositories. OMX is a Nordic Large Cap company in the Financial sector on the OMX Nordic Exchange.

For more information, please visit www.omxgroup.com

No. 1 in marketplace solutions

Calgary · Copenhagen · Dubai · Helsinki · Hong Kong · London · Milan · New York · Oslo · Reykjavik · Riga · Shanghai · Singapore · Stockholm · Sydney · Tallinn · Vilnius

Chapter six

Education and Market Regulation: Achieving an Equilibrium

Sound Regulation is about market dialogue, understanding the business and ensuring that ethics are upheld and fraud or money laundering closed off. Maintaining the confidence of the marketplace is vital, otherwise regulators will be seen as remote and hindering the markets' development.

The Exchange Manifesto

"What are the rules you need to know if you are moving from one country to another? What are the things that are compulsory in one country and forbidden in another? Common sense won't tell you. We have to tell each other."

Douglas Adams

In a world where electronic financial markets have exploded in a manner which is difficult for the average investor to appreciate, it is not surprising that certain lags exist.

Even amongst the G8 nations at the forefront of wholesale markets such as the UK and the USA, the collective ignorance of the population remains a subject for concern. In part this is a reflection of a media which itself has struggled to appreciate just how radically the world of finance has changed. Many newspapers and periodicals are still driven by advertising from those institutions who are keen to try to avoid overly emphasising the march of development as it may affect their short-term profitability usually affects their bottom line profits!

Nevertheless, the trickle down of education is a key effect for all markets and in the world of market development, it cannot be forgotten. In some nations, the statistics are quite literally staggering. Various Indian exchanges for instance are regularly educating a number greater than the entire population of Luxembourg on a quarterly basis! Nevertheless, there is often significant resistance to change in financial markets – and alas, the practitioners themselves are frequently one of the single most reactionary groups in that regard!

Any market, whether new or established, needs to have a regular dialogue with not merely its users but also all those who may be affected by its activities. To this end, government, the media and indeed regulators are a vital first step!

Many are those who simply have no idea about the bounteous opportunities afforded by the creation of more transparent market trading mechanisms for all types of product. Equally, exchanges have a very clear need to educate about the risks as well as the rewards. In a world of risks, it is clear that much damage can be wrought by those without driving licences driving cars on the highways, just as inexperienced traders can do significant damage to their own and others' financial health if they act in a foolish manner.

Of course, regulation plays a vital role in all financial markets. To that end, independent regulatory bodies are vitally important. However, regulation works best in dynamic financial markets when it is applied in a manner which permits the incredible ingenuity of the contemporary financial practitioner to flourish. In this respect, the old fashioned concept of rules based regulation seems to be dying out in many markets. Trying to create a rules based framework (let alone specific rules for every situation) is essentially impossible unless government is willing to devote vast resources to financial regulation. Even then, the resources may not have the desired effect and they are certainly resources which could be applied much more profitably to other aspects of government services.

The concept of modern regulation which needs to be espoused to ensure a dynamic and essentially safe dealing system is a system of principles based regulations. By having key principles which need to be adhered to, the concepts of fraud or ethics can be easily understood. In so doing, the financial marketplace can be free to expand rapidly. Moreover, the regulators, through nurturing good relationships with practitioners and encouraging open dialogue, will always have an opportunity to monitor markets while not being expected to be involved in the precise nuances of every single last action.

At the very building block stage, government must provide a sound rule of law, with enforceable debts on trading products. Exchanges ought to be entirely open to competition and not regarded as national chattels. Regulation which restricts the number of exchanges which can be licensed in any territory is protectionist and entirely counter-productive to market innovation. Similarly, exchange controls, or any other form of capital or currency movement restriction is akin to placing a "please don't invest here you're not welcome" sign on top of your nation's portion of the world map. Avoid subsidies too, they provide little benefit – as the South African Maize Board's abolition proved. If your country has a record of restrictions on capitalism then don't be surprised when it's the keen students of deregulation that win the prizes. Similarly, close your markets in any way and your population will eventually find the lure of fighting it out with North Korea at the bottom of the global misery indices largely unappealing.

Regulators are required to endeavour to ensure orderly markets to the best of their ability while equally providing a manner of protection against the least able investors who may be liable to exploitation. That said, the whole concept of investor protection remains somewhat of a minefield until regulators permit investors to be effectively graded (via education or experience) so that ultimately there can be a tier of "professional" investors who can trade in more or less whatever they choose.

Similarly, the process for regulators ought not to be in the business of deciding what products can be offered to clients. Let the market decide! Sensible regulated brokers and exchanges will not try to provide products they deem utterly inappropriate. Moreover, once regulators endeavour to restrict what product may be offered in a particular country, the product itself has an irritating habit of appearing offshore in some alternative vehicle which the regulator cannot remotely touch!

Sound Regulation is about market dialogue, understanding the business and ensuring that ethics are upheld and fraud or money laundering closed off. Maintaining the confidence of the marketplace is vital, otherwise regulators will be seen as remote and hindering the markets' development. These are the sorts of key principles that are at work in financial regulatory organisations in the United Kingdom and France for instance.

In this respect it may be difficult to recruit the most capable regulators as they are often likely to be paid much higher sums in the private sector. However, often it may be better to employ a few public-minded former practitioners on significant salaries than a large swathe of functionary bureaucrats.

Regulation is in any case a global issue. Through co-operation and sound mutual understanding, even the tiniest of financial centres can create a great body of intelligence and through judicious information exchange, learn a great deal about other arms of the companies they regulate and so on. To this end, regulators are thoroughly advised to partake of key fora such as the annual AFM gathering which is centred around the emerging world's exchanges.

When it comes to education and qualification, again a principles-based approach is by far the best. The notion of regulators asking hundreds of questions concerning the contract size of specific markets and so forth was frankly ludicrous in a world before the internet provided such information at our fingertips. Teach principles and monitor how the practitioners apply them. Similarly, for emerging marketplaces, be generous in your ability to "grandfather" experienced traders from elsewhere into your system. The insistence of some regimes that everybody must study for trading exams is frankly, silly. It smacks of the sort of belligerent Stalinist tactics that give regulators a bad name.

Finally, avoid predicting the next crash and regulate accordingly. Regulators have a record that trumps even Wall Street's collective economists when it comes to not spotting market collapses. The current score languishes around zero out of umpteen hundred crashes throughout history. The business of regulators is ensuring a simple, sensible, principled approach to organised markets. Writing endless rules may make work for less able regulators but it invariably does little to help markets – and above all in a globally interconnected world, he who regulates the most, loses the business to he whose light touch balances the business of regulation with an efficient, business-friendly environment. After all, if your regulators go over the top, there is always another jurisdiction ready to take advantage of the process.

Moreover, the whole business of trader education is one where the rules for trader exams need to be carefully considered. Keeping the bar fairly low for qualified individuals is a good idea. Making brokers demonstrate knowledge of ethics and good trading behaviour ought to be paramount. Vast exams asking facts that can be easily checked on the internet (such as contract sizes and so on) are just a waste of time for all parties concerned. True, traders must understand rules but then again creating rules that are so arcane they render any reader soporific within a few moments of being shown several hundreds of pages of manuals, is entirely counter-productive to growing a sound market and a sensible regulatory system.

Sound regulation is a partnership between regulator and practitioner. Communication is vital and the regulator must learn to get out of the way of new product that is aimed at experienced and professional investors. Indeed, regulators need to consider that the growth of a financial market system can only help secure their own job. After all, if a regulator doesn't allow a new product on their terrain, it only allows for a rival regulator in a neighbouring country to allow that product in and, hey presto, not only has the original nation lost a great opportunity but the regulator too has effectively reduced the future size of their market pool of folk to levy regulatory fees from.

A few years ago, I addressed a leading global regulators conference and mentioned various new products which, whether the regulators liked it or not (it was plain from their faces that many of them disliked even the vaguest notions of them intensely), these products were already gaining a foothold. Just as alcohol abolition spawned a wondrous industry, so too, not regulating product can spur a massive illicit trade which is arguably a lot more dangerous to the public's health as it is entirely unregulated. Anyway, the following day, a regulator from a populous emerging nation introduced me to the CEO of her national exchange over lunch. She had already telephoned him the previous evening to outline certain products as she was keen for him to consider listing as she could see their market potential. I must admit to having been somewhat surprised – keynote speeches don't always have such instant results, do they? The simple fact was that the regulator could see a potential for the product throughout her continent and as she said to me afterwards, she felt her agency was the most capable of actually regulating the product – therefore she wanted to suggest it to her national exchange in the hope their country would gain an economic advantage.

Now that's what regulation ought to be about...

CENTRAL CLEARING HOUSE AND DEPOSITORY (BUDAPEST) LTD.

CSD services
- Maintenance of central securities database
- Allocation of ISINs
- Dematerialization
- (Central) securities account management
- Book-entry operations
- Corporate actions

CCP services
- Clearing and settlement of guaranteed Exchange transactions
- Clearing and settlement of off-Exchange transactions
- Cash account management

Other services
- Cross-border clearing and settlement
- Registry and paying agent services

CONTACT DETAILS

Mr. Tamás Madlena
Director
Marketing & Customer Relations
Tel: +36 (1) 483 - 6274
madlena.tamas@keler.hu

Mr. Áron Varga

Marketing & Customer Relations
Tel: +36 (1) 483 - 6275
varga.aron@keler.hu

Address: KELER Ltd., 1075 Budapest, Asboth u. 9-11., Hungary
Tel: +36 (1) 483 - 6100 • Fax: +36 (1) 342 - 3539
www.keler.hu • keler@keler.hu

Chapter seven

Competition - Prospects and Development

For those who think that financial market competition has already reached fever pitch, this chapter will be riddled with a somewhat perverse sense of disappointment. For, ladies and gentlemen, the marketplace has only completed its limbering up exercises.

The Exchange Manifesto

"Most executives would like to believe that they're in charge of their organisations, that they make the crucial decisions and that when they decide that something should be done everyone snaps to and executes...in practice, it is a company's customers who effectively control what it can and cannot do."

Clayton M. Christensen

For those who think that financial market competition has already reached fever pitch, this chapter will be riddled with a somewhat perverse sense of disappointment. For, ladies and gentlemen, the marketplace has only completed its limbering up exercises. The impact of deregulation is enormous and growing. The technological impact on markets is simply incredible and there is no sign that it will stop revolutionising the market process.

As things stand, the whole concept of an asset class is changing. To that end, the process of product development is moving into what is the greatest golden age ever seen to date. This is driven by the rapid development and deployment of global electronic platforms throughout the past decade. New product is already expanding vastly whether it is in new areas such as emissions and weather or through old established debt and equity markets with ever more intriguing structured products and so on.

Similarly, the business of exchanges is moving apace. At the very top end of the business the oft mooted consolidation of exchanges will continue and the likelihood of a few key powerhouse markets in the USA and Europe (indeed Trans-Atlantic markets even) is in the process of emerging. Nevertheless, the prospects for smaller exchanges have never been so bright. Admittedly, exchanges need to be brave – and here it has to be said, traditionally small exchanges demonstrate a cowardice for making radical decisions which puts them on a par with the worst weasels of middle management the world over.

The Exchange Manifesto

There are wars to be won and to the victor the spoils! The tragedy for many exchanges is that it won't be the challenge they rise to that kills them. Rather the tragedy is that the smaller markets which die will often do so because they cowered at the prospect of rising to the challenge and eventually went under, forgotten as victims of the crossfire.

The microexchange – the very tiniest of exchanges with a minuscule secretariat and often only an extremely modest initial market activity (either a regional market or a local segment) - seemed to have died in the wake of the dotcom bubble's explosive demise at the start of this century. However, as technology has become ever cheaper, in fact the imperative for the microexchange has grown ever stronger. Specialist companies such as COMDAQ can manufacture software solutions for tiny exchanges (the Nepal Stock Exchange for instance whose "Big Bang" COMDAQ powered in 2007) have become ever cheaper and therefore the ability to create micro-markets becomes ever simpler.

Meanwhile, every single aspect of financial markets remains at risk and to that end the prospect for exchange platforms to even do simple processes such as the borrowing and lending traditionally undertaken by banks remains significant too. The likes of Zopa have created loan exchanges to revolutionise the business of borrowing and lending for many.

With the ability to securitise just about any conceivable asset, the prospects for markets are simply huge. Likewise the prospects for exchanges are little short of enormous. The business of the exchange marketplace will grow enormously in the coming decades as the delineation between all forms of products narrows. Already exchange markets have seen the rise of the likes of Alibaba and eBay which are to all intents and purposes exchanges. The key challenge for governments, politicians, regulators, entrepreneurs and practitioners is to create an ongoing wave of new markets which can help make commerce simpler, more efficient, frictionless and at the same time provide greater prosperity which can reach every corner of the globe and provide a sustainable commercial future in harmony with local custom and the local environment wherever business is done.

The challenge awaits, the results can benefit us all.

Deutsche Börse Systems

Powering Xetra®, Eurex® & the Market Data, Risk Management, Clearing and Settlement Systems of Deutsche Börse Group & Partners

"Russian Trading System" Stock Exchange – the mirror of the Russian economy

RTS was established in 1995 to consolidate separate regional securities trading floors into a unified regulated Russian securities market. RTS lists leading Russian securities that are of great interest to both domestic and foreign portfolio investors, thus providing the industry with the most important market indicators.

RTS encompasses two centralized stock markets – Classic and T+0 Market, the system of indicative quotation of securities RTS Board, FORTS (Futures & Options on RTS) derivatives market and over-the-counter FX market RTS Money.

RTS Classic Market is the only trading platform in Russia that allows settlement in foreign currency. Access to RTS Classic Market is equally accessible by both Russian and foreign investors. The main advantage of the Classic market is the absence of the requirement to deposit securities and cash assets before the beginning of trading. RTS Classic market data is used in calculation of RTS Index, the main indicator of Russian securities market.

T+0 market is equally accessible to both large-scale and small investors through all kinds of Internet trading systems (orders are submitted through the Gateway). Trading is performed in the order-driven mode with full preliminary deposition on assets; settlement is conducted in rubles using the "delivery versus payment" technology.

FORTS (Futures and Options on RTS) is the leading Russian derivatives market. It gives all types of investors a widest range of possibilities to hedge risks on the securities and currency markets and to perform arbitrage in derivatives contracts. FORTS product line includes the contracts on RTS Index, "blue chips", interest rates, US dollar exchange rate and commodities. The future contracts on gold application has begun with oil and oil products trading on commodity market FORTS. In perspective future contracts on agricultural products are to be introduced.

RTS Index, the official Exchange indicator first calculated on September 1, 1995, has since become the benchmark in Russian securities industry. The index is computed on thirty-minute intervals using real-time prices of the 50 most liquid stocks listed on the Exchange and is relayed to the RTS Web site (www.rts.ru), RTS workstations and news agencies.

"Russian Trading System" Stock Exchange
127006, Russia, Moscow, Dolgorukovskaya Str. 38, bld.1
+7 495 705 90 31 (phone), +7 495 733 97 03 (fax)
info@rts.ru, www.rts.ru

Chapter eight

Conclusion

There are wars to be won and to the victor the spoils! The tragedy for many exchanges is that it won't be the challenge they rise to that kills them. Rather the tragedy is that the markets which die will often do so because they cowered at the prospect of rising to the challenge and eventually went under, forgotten as victims of the crossfire.

The Exchange Manifesto

"Rules by their very nature are simple. Our problem is not the complexity of our models but the far greater complexity of a world economy whose underlying linkages appear to be in a continual state of flux."
Alan Greenspan

"You don't tax a loss, you only tax a profit. We're all in this together."
Enoch Powell

Exchanges are the best means of creating widespread credible markets and ultimately pushing prosperity to every element of society. Open market approaches provide the best possible opportunity at the lowest cost for governments to encourage the development of economies the world over.

I wrote this book driven by a pure passion for markets. The modern electronic exchange mechanism is the best means available to humanity to improve its economic prospects. The benefits are not only economic. After all emissions trading can reduce the harmful effects of industrial production. Moreover, the exchange operates on a basis of both collective and individual self interest, thus ensuring that everybody can have the chance to operate within the marketplace on reasonable terms. Exchanges are just a simple extension of the markets which have been formed around barter and trade since the beginning of not just civilisation but indeed primitive cultures too.

The concept behind this book was not to provide a comprehensive guide to what needs to be done to create or develop exchanges. Rather, it has been produced as a pocket sized manifesto for the exchange marketplace. In that sense, it is intended to provide a succinct and readable review of the world of exchanges and how they affect commerce throughout the world, particularly within the world's many emerging markets.

The Exchange Manifesto

It has been driven by the desire of the Association of Futures Markets to have a book which while not their policies per se, at least encapsulates many of their core precepts. I wrote this book out of passion to see the world of exchanges better understood throughout the world. Therefore we hope this slim volume will have whetted your appetite to learn more about exchanges and to exploit their many advantages to benefit all mankind.

The world will continue to see more expansion in financial markets and financial centres in the coming decades. The business of exchanges while there may be many mergers and takeovers, will nonetheless continue to support a multitude of different products and platforms. It is important that new markets can be opened whether they want to trade fine wines, food products or whatever! The modern electronic exchange – even a low budget MicroExchange, can be created to take advantage of a niche locally, nationally, regionally or even globally. In that respect the exchange is an agent of the sort of global marketplace which can only help promote development.

As markets morph, so too will exchanges be a pivotal part of their development. Nevertheless, there will be casualties and many will need to be brave if they are to take the risks they need to prosper in their niche. To the loser, the likely future is oblivion. Never forget that some cities on the Silk Road were not merely bypassed as trade routes changed, the entire cities themselves fell into disrepair and in fact disappeared off the map!

No matter what size an exchange is the mantra must be:
• Be Brave, Be Fast and Be Willing to Innovate.

The message to government and regulators must be:
• Have Faith, Be Fast and Be Competitive.

To everyone else, I would say, look to the future of the exchange for within you will find a way to change the world and make our lives richer in many ways that prosperity can be measured.

Vive La Revolution!
Prosperity for All!

Patrick L Young
Monaco
May 1st, 2007

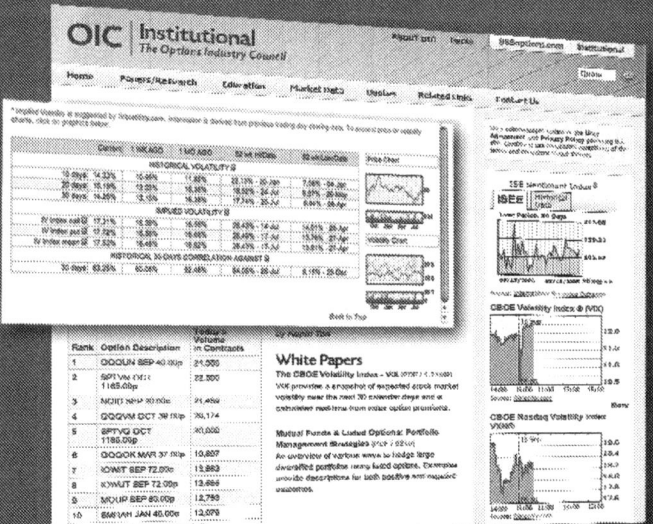

About the author:

Patrick L Young

Patrick L Young is a leading independent thinker on capital market structure, having authored several books including the acclaimed "Capital Market Revolution!" His analyses have proven consistently prescient in their prognosis of developments in everything from fees through stock exchange structure, new product groups and the rise of hedge funds (etc.) to the use of technology.

A passionate innovator, he has been in the vanguard of introducing new products such as Single Stock Futures and creating exchanges for the trading of contracts on Sports and Entertainment markets. He is currently working on a series of new market applications.

He has in the past consulted to many leading organisations throughout the world. He is represented by AESX, BESA, CME, Deutsche Börse, EOEX, EUREX, Euronext, IPE, LIFFE, Montreal Exchange, SAFEX as well as many major banks/investment banks, fund managers and government organisations.

Patrick remains a sought after speaker at conferences throughout the world, he is represented by Celebrity Speakers Agency, having keynoted for audiences of up to 1000 people throughout the world.

Patrick is a regular guest on CNBC Europe and a media commentator in leading financial journals and digital media, including the FT, Wall Street Journal and Australian Financial Review, having broadcast on BBC, Bloomberg, CNN, ITV and Reuters as well as networks in Belgium, Germany, Hong Kong, Italy, Switzerland and the USA.

Patrick@DerivativesVision.com

Further Reading:

Patrick L Young:

- Capital Market Revolution! (FT Prentice Hall 1999)
- New Capital Market Revolution (Texere 2002)
- The Promiscuous Investor (erivatives 2001)

White papers:

- Megatrends in Finance (Detica 2006)
- Towards A TransAtlantic Tiger (Derivatives Vision 2006)
- Product Development (from FESE conference, 2006)

By other authors:

- Market Unbound: Unleashing Global Capitalism (Hardcover)
  by Lowell Brian and Diana Farrell (John Wiley & Sons, 1996)
- Confusión de Confusiones: ("Confusion of Confusions")
  by Joseph de La Vega (Sonsbeek Publishers 2006)
- The Frontiers of Fortune
  by Jonathan Story (FT Prentice Hall, 1999)
- Banker to the Poor
  by Muhammad Yunus (PublicAffairs 2003)"

Periodicals:

- The Economist
- Monocle

Printed in the United kingdom
by Lightening Source UK Ltd.
118418UK00001B/34-111

www.ingramcontent.com/pod-product-compliance
Ingram Content Group UK Ltd.
Pitfield, Milton Keynes, MK11 3LW, UK
UKHW041419180426
11947UKWH00007B/219